CHRIST
and the
New Consciousness

John P. Newport

BROADMAN PRESS
Nashville, Tennessee

Dedicated to
Harry and Hazel Chavanne
Friends of Vision and Concern

4266-04
ISBN: 0-8054-6604

Dewey Decimal Classification: 291
Subject headings: SECTS // CONSCIOUSNESS GROUPS //
CHRISTIANITY AND OTHER RELIGIONS

Library of Congress Catalog Card Number: 77-78621
Printed in the United States of America

Preface

The New Consciousness revolution is a continuing fact of modern times. There are many perspectives from which the New Consciousness developments can be approached, including descriptive, negative, sympathetic, and evaluative.

Two developments in my teaching career while doing research for this study have fostered diverse approaches. For a number of years I taught in America's largest graduate theological seminary, Southwestern Baptist. Southwestern is a professional school preparing men and women for Christian ministry. Although the descriptive approach was utilized, evaluation was ultimately made on the basis of a Christian presupposition. In 1976, I became Chavanne Professor of Religious Studies at Rice University, an academically-oriented secular university. In this context, the emphasis is placed on the descriptive approach. *Christ and the New Consciousness* utilizes the descriptive approach. In addition, it seeks to evaluate the New Consciousness revolution in both a positive and negative manner from the perspective of Evangelical Christianity. There are lessons to be learned as well as judgments to be made.

Material found in this study has been developed in relation to lectures and addresses at various colleges, universities, layman's meetings, and churches. I am especially grateful to the Staley Foundation for the opportunity to present lectureships under their auspices.

Mr. Richard O'Keeffe and the staff of Fondren Library, Rice University, have been especially helpful in the preparation of this volume. Professor Niels Nielson of Rice University must be singled out for words of gratitude. Appreciation must also be given to Nancy Desmond, my secretary, who has been both an efficient typist and an intelligent critic. Undergirding all that I try to do is my wife, Eddie Belle, who is a constant source of inspiration and encouragement.

John P. Newport
Houston, Texas

Contents

Introduction

Jean Houston, a dynamic professor from New York City, spoke to a group of Texas students on the New Consciousness explosion. Sitting in the back of the room, I noted the students' affirmative response as Professor Houston outlined the development of this new approach to reality in America. She suggested that this alternative development has taken place against the background of a culture which to many seems dehumanized and overrationalized.

In the midst of the 1960s, I went to the Haight-Ashbury area in San Francisco and to the campus of the University of California at Berkeley. I wanted to observe firsthand the dynamics of this New Consciousness or counterculture movement. Later I visited Greenwich Village in New York City to note similar developments. In these counterculture centers I found young people looking for new ways to feel and know. Traditional approaches associated with the biblical way were seen as too closely aligned with that which impaired life. There was a reaction against technocracy, traditional educational methods in the universities, and middle-class patterns of life.

The first stage of the rise of the New Consciousness movement was emotional and essentially irrational. All America heard of the "love, peace, and groovy" flower children. Timothy Leary, discharged Harvard professor, told the first wave of counterculture young people of ways to find reality and religious experience through LSD and other drugs. Music and meditation were features of love-ins, be-ins, and rock festivals. If there was interest in the Christian tradition, it was in terms of new styles emphasizing speaking in tongues or "last days" predictions.[1]

Charles Glock, of the University of California, contends that the appearance of these dramatic New Consciousness groups is only the surfacing of a new mode of consciousness that has been slowly developing for decades.[2] Jeanne Messer suggests that the New Consciousness groups are the vanguard of a new approach to reality, a symbolic transformation in the West. For Messer, traditional Western religious forms, at least in the manner they have been taught and expressed, have run their course.[3] According to Edward Tiryakian, the New Consciousness groups are not an ephemeral fad but a part of the formation of a new cultural approach to

7

reality. They constitute a major happening.[4]

J. Stillson Judah maintains that Americans have associated traditional Hebrew-Christian ways of religious expression with a certain type of life-style. This life-style is characterized by American "don't care" individualism, a passion for material success and technology. Such a way of life is seen as resulting in pollution, the abuse of natural resources, and the alienation of humans from the environment, others, and themselves.[5]

THE CHRIST-CONSCIOUSNESS—YESTERDAY AND TODAY

As I listened to Jean Houston of the Foundation of Mind Research Center speak of the emergence of the New Consciousness groups, several thoughts came into my mind. I recalled my visits to Berkeley and Greenwich Village and the statements of Glock and Judah. I sought to put all of these experiences into the context of my own religious experience and training.

As a college student on a national debate tour, I visited university campuses in most of the eastern part of the United States. Trip plans called for us to spend much time in fraternity houses. After six weeks of observation and conversation, I was repulsed by the philosophy and perspective of many of the students. Drinking styles, sexual exploits, and the quick buck were primary topics of conversation. Subconsciously I knew that there had to be a better or more fulfilling life-style or life purpose. As a graduation gift, I was given a trip to a national youth conference. In positive and exciting terms and life-styles, the dynamics of the biblical and Christian way of life were presented. It was a refreshing and inviting alternative to what I had experienced in my earlier college life. Later, in a more scholastic setting, I studied the impact that Christ and Christianity made in the early Graeco-Roman world and in subsequent history.

For students of religious history, it is well known that Christ lived and taught in a time of religious change and crisis similar to today. The background of Christ's ministry was complex. Some people in his time were attracted to the one God concept and to the demands of the Hebrew religion. Others found the secret initiations of the mystery religions, with their dying-rising gods, meaningful. The universalism of Stoicism was widely acclaimed. The great nature and fertility gods were continuing in their influence.

Christ and Christianity provided a new consciousness in that era. In the Christian understanding of the cross and resurrection, the early Christians found that they could participate in a saving death-and-rebirth experience more profound than that of any mystery religion.

After Christ's resurrection and appearance and the coming of the Holy

Spirit at Pentecost, his disciples were vitalized and dynamized. They went out to proclaim that the Jesus who had taught, died, and arose was Lord and Messiah. They told the Graeco-Roman world that the Old Testament prophecies about the Jewish and universal roles of the Messiah and the last days were fulfilled in Jesus. In fact, they excitedly preached that the new age, when the reign of the Jewish God would be evident everywhere, was already present in Christ.[6]

The message was given to a Jewish believer, Paul, who proclaimed the full universalism of Jesus. The apostle Paul told the Gentiles that they could be grafted into the spiritual tree originally constituted by the Jews. As Gentiles, they did not have to follow the detailed ritual laws of Moses. Christ's death on the cross broke the sway of sin and death and overcame legalism. In his resurrection Jesus Christ brought life to all men.

The Christian religion made available a new consciousness to the Mediterranean world of the first century. Rich and poor, slave and free, and humble and mighty embraced this dynamic new religion.[7] Christianity superseded the Neoplatonic mysticism favored by the philosophers. It succeeded the Mithraism popular in the Roman army. It took the place of the worship of many gods upheld by traditional Roman leaders.[8]

In the twentieth century, people continue to find an exciting life-style and a personal consciousness-heightening in the Christian way centering in the person of Jesus Christ. Consequently it is difficult for Christian believers to understand the significance of a statement by Theodore Roszak that the hope of the West is in a synthesis of the non-Christian New Consciousness groups.[9]

THE CHRISTIAN RESPONSE TO THE RISE OF NEW CONSCIOUSNESS GROUPS

A study of the New Consciousness groups is important, however, for the Christian as well as other people interested in vital spiritual development. Involved is our own personal spiritual future as well as the welfare of our culture. Although the New Consciousness groups are often presented in modernized and updated forms, they represent the religious thinking of over one half of the people of the globe.

Most of the New Consciousness groups prominent today stem from age-long traditions rooted in the Far East, the Middle East, and Africa. Transcendental Meditation, for example, is a modernizing and updating of an ancient thirteenth century Hindu philosophy or religion. Nichiren Shoshu is rooted in Japanese Buddhism. Est utilizes Zen Buddhist insights.

Evangelical and conservative Christians tend to respond to the growth

9

of the New Consciousness groups in different ways.

Some see the New Consciousness development—especially the darker side such as magic and witchcraft—as a direct fulfillment of biblical prophecy. From this perspective, the growth of these groups is a visible manifestation of the work of Satan which is predicted in the Bible for the very last period of history.[10]

Many of the New Consciousness groups are seen as a fulfillment of the vision of John's Revelation of an ultimate antichrist kingdom at the end of history. This kingdom is seen as embracing false religious worship, occult gnosis, and psychic power. John called it the "Mystery of Babylon." Mankind is being brought together in the last days of history in a common expression of humanistic "spirituality." The esoteric core of the ancient Babylonian gnosis is similar to many forms of Eastern and occult mysticism. Today this mysticism is called Yoga, Illumination, or the "Divine Principle" (Sun Myung Moon).

Other evangelical Christians see the New Consciousness groups as constituting a situation similar to that of the time of Christ. In the first century, the mystery religions, the worship of Greek and Roman gods, and Greek philosophies aroused the people to reflect on ultimate questions. In a similar way today the New Consciousness groups are revealing the limitations of scientism and secularism as ultimate world views, and are forcing people to think of life's central spiritual concerns. It was "In the fulness of time" that Christ came in the first century. From this perspective the New Consciousness groups are helping to constitute a new fullness of time for a fresh restatement of the Christian way.

A number of years ago I began attending International Student conferences each Thanksgiving. As representatives of Far Eastern and Middle Eastern groups spoke or shared their views, I was aroused to study the latent resources in the Christian faith that had been neglected or covered over. Organized Christianity in its institutional and intellectual forms tends to harden and identify too readily with prevalent cultural developments. Observant Christian leaders emphasize that an authentic religion must be in a continual renewal and reformation experience. Some sensitive leaders see the New Consciousness groups as challenging Christian groups to continue such a renewal and reformation.

In a country which grants the right of religious liberty and freedom of religious proclamation, people need extensive knowledge and insight as a basis for discrimination. Concerned Christians should seek to understand the dynamics and teachings of the New Consciousness groups. Similarities and differences between these groups and the biblical tradition should be noted Reasons for the growth and popularity of the New

Consciousness groups should be carefully analyzed. Equipped with such knowledge and insight, the Christian and other interested people will have a background for understanding, dialogue, witness, and criticism.

In this study an attempt will be made to present the background, key personalities, central ideas, and dynamics of representative New Consciousness groups. From a secular perspective, positive and negative evaluations will be made. Finally, evaluations from a Christian or theological perspective will be noted.

The New Consciousness groups represent a wide spectrum of groups and personalities. It will be helpful to see these groups as they are rooted in their native spiritual and cultural soil. Many of them are updated adaptations of age-long traditions. The classifications which we shall use are somewhat arbitrary, but they should bring some order to what appears to be a chaotic assortment of groups.

PART ONE
Hindu-related New Consciousness Groups
1
Hinduism Comes West

In the 1950s I caught the first stirrings of the New Consciousness revolution while living in Cambridge, Massachusetts. Huston Smith of the Massachusetts Institute of Technology was attracting large groups of students to his classes and lectures on the Far Eastern Religions. Robert Slater was helping to establish a center for the study of World Religions at Harvard. Both of these scholars agreed that the roots of most of the New Consciousness groups were to be found in India.

In order to better understand these roots, in the 1960s I went to the Hindu pilgrimage city of Banaras, India. My visit there was an unforgettable experience of study and consultation. Since that time I have returned to India with study groups and have seen the flowering of the New Consciousness groups whose roots are in ancient India.

Many Westerners are looking to the East and India for a New Consciousness turn on. If careful study is made, Westerners will find that behind the updated Hindu groups is a new world view and life-style that is radically different from the classic biblical view of the West.[1]

The sacred scriptures upon which modern Hinduism is based, the Vedas, are written in Sanskrit and are thought to be at least three thousand years old. These ancient writings speak of many deities, all of whom are manifestations of Brahman, or god. Other sacred writings, such as the *Bhagavad Gita* (Song of the Lord), celebrate devotion to an incarnation of Brahman, lord Krishna, and praise the discipline of Yoga.

The religious philosophy of India reached high points in the ninth and twelfth centuries after Christ. Perhaps the most basic intellectual philosophy of India, known as Vedanta, was developed by Shankara in the ninth century A.D. A more personal approach was developed by the bhakti movement in the twelfth century A.D.[2]

The Hindu religion was relatively dormant until it was aroused in direct reaction to evangelical Christian missionaries such as William Carey in the early nineteenth century. In 1893 the first Parliament on World Religions was held in Chicago. The star of the show was a humble Hindu known as Swami Vivekenanda. From that time on Hinduism became attractive to many American and European intellectuals such as Aldous

Huxley and Christopher Isherwood.

From 1918 until 1946 various Hindu spiritual leaders such as Yogananda lectured and formed groups in the United States. After World War II, especially in the 1960s, there was a literal explosion of Hindu gurus or religious teachers appearing on the American scene. Discounting heavy intellectualism, these gurus emphasized a direct turning on to spiritual reality. Light, color, incense, music, and touch were widely used to induce religious experience.[3]

These new Hindu groups took to an extreme the basic New Consciousness idea that the only god one can find is within. Words are seen as secondary to an atmosphere which ignites the interior experience. When words are used, it is usually in a chanting or repetitive way. Turning from social concerns, the new Hindu groups emphasized the individual's inner spiritual development by means of meditation, Yoga, chanting, and demonstrations of love for one another. Charismatic gurus offered specific techniques and methods of spiritual awareness. Some disciples became aggressively missionary and were characterized by enthusiasm and determination. The mass media as well as books and magazines were used to share their optimistic messages.[4]

There are significant differences in organization and practices among Hindu New Consciousness groups. The root world view, as indicated above, which underlies most Hindu groups is known as Vedanta or pantheistic monism. This view undergirds the thought of Transcendental Meditation as well as some Buddhist groups. Hare Krishna modifies the more abstract Vedanta view by declaring that reality is more personal.[5]

2
Hinduism in a Nutshell

It is an intellectual adventure to enter the world of Hinduism. An understanding of certain basic Hindu concepts will help us to get into contemporary Hindu New Consciousness groups.

BRAHMAN (GOD)

Ultimate or absolute reality for Hinduism is known as *Brahman*. Brahman or god is absolute existence, absolute consciousness, and absolute bliss. It is impersonal. It is above all distinctions and is beyond thought.

For a practical, nonphilosophical person who cannot conceive of an impersonal spirit, Brahman is seen as the originator or creator of a semi-real world. But for the "enlightened" person this world is unreal and a mere illusion. Brahman alone is real.

Brahman is not a personal transcendent being and therefore cannot be offended. Sin for the Hindu is essentially an ignorance that prevents a person from realizing his oneness with god. Failure to achieve enlightenment in this life means that a person will have to undergo rebirth.[6]

MAYA (THE NATURE OF THE WORLD)

If Brahman or Unity alone is real, then what about the ordinary world we know? For Vedanta Hinduism, it is a dream. The dreamer (god) is real but his dream is unreal. This dream world is called *maya*. The world of science and everyday existence is illusion, ignorance, and shadow. It is a world where individuality and diversity are *thought* to be real but actually they are not. Only those of us who are ignorant consider the world to be real. When you are enlightened, you will realize the world is illusory and only Brahman is real. This is called Absolute Idealism. Christian Science has a somewhat similar idea in its teaching that "God is Spirit, God is All, God is Love. There is no evil, sin, sickness, death or matter. They are the delusion of the mortal mind."

Recognized scientists and philosophers such as A. N. Whitehead contend that this view of maya has hindered India in terms of progress in science and technology. The East, many suggest, could never have given birth to modern science as it is known in the West. The Hindu view of maya also makes it difficult to distinguish between fantasy and reality.[7]

ATMAN (MAN'S NATURE)

Who is man? What is man? Since everything is Brahman or god, man must be identical with god or a part of god, from the Hindu perspective.

The average Westerner sees himself as composed of body, mind, and soul or self. For Hinduism, the body and mind, like other material objects, are merely illusory appearances. When this is realized, the only reality that remains is *atman* or self. This self is nothing other than Brahman or god.

When you are unenlightened or ignorant, you associate the self with the body. In this state you are in bondage and act like a finite, limited creature.

Liberation or enlightenment is reached through the realization of the self's identity with god or Brahman. The way to liberation is to come under the tutelage of a master or guru who has himself realized his divinity or Brahman.[8]

The *true self* is god. The *I* which I consider myself to be is in reality the *not-self*. This not-self is caught in a world of illusion, ignorance and bondage. Yoga is the liberation of the not-self to allow it to be absorbed back into god.[9]

Salvation is thus a matter of realizing what we already are rather than becoming what we should be. You must lose your personal ego-consciousness into god. You must say, "I am Brahman."

This retreat from individuality is openly emphasized as a Hindu ideal for life. After a time in marriage and business, the normal Hindu is expected to retreat into spiritual meditation. Exceptional men often leave everyday life much earlier and often totally abandon wife, family, and business as did Gautama Buddha. The Hindu view tends to create a pessimistic attitude toward the value of individuality in life. Alan Watts describes man as the "ego-mask." [10]

This notion of atman is at diametrical odds with the biblical view. For the Bible, personality is the chief attribute of God and the foremost attribute of man.

KARMA (LAW OF RETRIBUTION)

Karma is the Hindu teaching that one's present life is the result of a past action in a former existence. It is related to the idea of reincarnation. Reincarnation follows from the general principle that nothing that is real (self or soul) ever passes out of existence. It may take many rebirths through centuries to finally be reabsorbed into Brahman but a soul or self will never pass into nonexistence.[11]

The law of karma is ironclad. There is no confession or forgiveness. The sin must be worked out. The soul will have to suffer later.

REINCARNATION AND IMMORTALITY

No man in the sense of an individual or person survives death. Atman or soul survives, but atman is impersonal. When atman is reincarnated, it becomes another person. There is immortality but it is not personal and individual.

GURU (SPIRITUAL TEACHER)

The guru or spiritual leader is the one appointed to help deliver you from your individuality. You must be led to merge with the absolute. Cults develop around those charismatic gurus who are most successful in leading disciples to god-realization. In fact, the *Upanishads,* Hindu holy scriptures, teach that true progress toward self-realization is not possible without the guidance and help of a guru. He alone is qualified to grant initiation and prescribe the spiritual discipline (sadhana) needed for each seeker. A person must completely submit to his guru's direction.

The gurus use various techniques. Sometimes they will give the disciple a secret *mantra,* which is a sacred word or formula. The disciple is told that he will realize a complete change in his character by meditating upon and repeating the mantra. Other gurus recommend meditation on a *mandala.* A mandala is a highly structured, often ornate, circular image, a symbol of the totality of reality. Alternate methods require the repetition of prayers and acts of obedience.

All of these techniques seek to get a person on the vibration level with Brahman. The ultimate goal is to become a part of the nondual, ultimate vibration—Brahman, or the one. It is easy to see how respect for a guru can evolve into a type of devotion similar to that given to God.[12]

AVATAR (GOD APPEARING AS MAN)

The average person in India cannot completely understand the idea of Brahman. Furthermore, it is not satisfying because it is too impersonal and abstract. A reform movement in the twelfth century developed the idea of Hindu gods as personal. Loving devotion to one or more of these gods is called *bhakti,* or adoration.

From time to time, when the need is great, these gods descend to earth in terms of an avatar or incarnation. The appearance of an avatar is unlike the birth of Jesus. An avatar, such as lord Krishna, oftentimes appears in the world in a divine form, looking like a human child, but in reality he is not human.

Some of the more contemporary Hindu New Consciousness groups see their founders as divine but having certain human qualities. In fact, some founders of groups are revealed as avatars in a dramatic manner. Sometimes it is the bite of a scorpion or the kiss of another great master which reveals an avatar. The revelation is usually followed by a public announcement of his divinity or avatar status.[13]

SAD-GURU (PERFECT MASTER)

When god becomes man, as we have seen, he is called an avatar, a god-man or messiah. While the divine may "descend" into the human level, a human may also "ascend" into the divine. This is done through mastery over his nature and an achieved union with god. When man thus becomes god he is called Sad-Guru or Perfect Master.

Although the Sad-Gurus obviously retain their bodies during earthly existence, these Perfect Masters are not conscious of their bodies. They claim to experience continually the bliss, power, and knowledge of god. A few of these masters choose to remain on earth and help other souls realize god. There are fifty-six god-realized souls in the world at all times, according to one version of Hindu teaching. Most of them work apart from the general public. Five masters, who constitute the directing body, always work in public.[14]

SADHANA (SPIRITUAL DISCIPLINE)

Each guru prescribes a discipline for his followers. If faithfully followed, this discipline should lead to god-realization, or samadhi (a mystic trance). Steps such as restraint, observances, posture, breath regulation, concentration, and meditation are utilized to lead to this god-realization. Different groups employ variations of the generally accepted techniques.

MANTRA (SACRED SOUND)

To properly understand some of the Hindu New Consciousness groups, one must realize the importance of sound in Hindu thought. Sounds can create and destroy. For certain Hindus the world is created and maintained by the utterance of proper sounds. These sacred sounds are called mantras. A mantra is a sound structure of one or more syllables which represents a particular aspect of the divine. They are revealed to men by religious leaders.

A mantra is not just a formula or prayer. It is an embodiment in sound of a particular god. It is god itself. Since the mantra is god in sound, it

17

must be repeated in the form revealed by the guru. It cannot be learned from books, but only from the voice of a living guru. Its mystic meaning is explained at the time of initiation into the group. The frequent repetition of the mantra will gradually transform the personality of the worshiper into that of the deity worshiped.[15]

As we shall see, mantras are very important in Transcendental Meditation and Hare Krishna, as well as in other Hindu New Consciousness groups. In fact, the heart of the work of Maharishi Mahesh Yogi and Transcendental Meditation is chanting or repeating a mantra.

YOGA (LIBERATION)

Yoga can be understood as a broad term including any aspect of Hinduism leading to self-liberation or god-realization. It is a practical system of self-culture developed by the ancient religious leaders of India. It is probably the world's oldest science of physical and mental self-development. It is the spiritualization of all of life. The various postures and breath controls are aids to spiritual realization. It seeks to make man's physical and emotional systems into instruments of spiritualized realization.

Yoga has come to America—even to men's health clubs. Recently I joined a downtown health club. The first sign I noticed directed people to the "Al Dugan Meditation Room." Al Dugan, an independent oil operator, is typical of the Westerners who have been attracted to Yoga. He now teaches a class in Yoga. Such a study begins with postures that streamline the figure. More serious students are led into meditation, concentration, and the quest for enlightenment. This impact of Yoga in America is a remarkable phenomenon.

As a means of uniting the individual soul with God, a number of spiritual paths have been developed under the Yoga umbrella. The one to be chosen for a particular person depends on a person's temperament and interests.

A. KARMA YOGA

Karma Yoga is for the activist—it is a way of works. The highest expression of Karma Yoga is service to others. Action in the world is not in itself a form of Yoga, but if it is carried on unselfishly with a view to helping others, then it is Karma Yoga.

Good karma takes a person nearer enlightenment; bad karma results in a lower stage in the next incarnation.

B. BHAKTI YOGA

Bhakti Yoga is for persons of a devotional temperament. It is the most

18

significant way for many of the New Consciousness groups. It involves love and devotion to god, to a spiritual teacher, or to divine incarnation.

Those in Bhakti Yoga recite god's glory, sing of god's qualities, and repeat mantras. It includes withdrawing the senses from worldly activity and seeing the whole world as god. One on this path is to be indifferent to pleasure or pain. Bhakti Yoga is the nearest Hinduism gets to a personal relationship with god.

C. JAPA YOGA

Japa Yoga is sometimes isolated as a separate path. It calls for the repetition of mantras or the name of the lord. When one repeats the name Rama or Krishna, for example, the likeness of Rama or Krishna will come to mind. For the person on this path such a recitation is seen as the cure for mankind's ills.

D. JNANA YOGA

Jnana Yoga is for the intellectual type. It is a way of knowledge and wisdom. Self-analysis and awareness are emphasized. It involves discrimination, indifference to sensual objects, and calmness of mind as ways of completely identifying with the divinity within.[16]

E. HATHA YOGA

Hatha Yoga is the physical yoga of breathing and postures. This is the path best known to Westerners. Followers claim that through bodily postures and mental concentration, health can be attained. Proper breathing will bring oxygen to the bloodstream. Concentration on specific nerve centers will restore vital energy.[17]

It is noteworthy that recognized Hindu leaders insist that Hatha or physical Yoga, according to classical definitions, is inherently and functionally related to Hindu philosophy. Classic commentaries on Yoga issue dire warnings for those who practice Hatha Yoga for purely physical ends, outside of a total context of spiritual discipline. This emphasis should be noted by those who teach Y.M.C.A. or church educational classes in Yoga for purely physical reasons.

F. TANTRA YOGA

Tantra Yoga focuses on ritualized sexual union as an end to union with Brahman.

G. KUNDALINI YOGA

Kundalini Yoga seeks to draw power for enlightenment up through centers of power in the body called chakras.

3
Transcendental Meditation (T.M.)

A large civic auditorium in Houston, Texas, was packed. The audience, mostly young adults, waited expectantly for the program personality, Maharishi Mahesh Yogi, founder and leader of Transcendental Meditation, to appear. At last he came on the stage in an ornate robe and went to sit on a throne-like chair on the platform. The audience arose in an attitude of rapt reverence.

Before the Maharishi was introduced as "his holiness," a Harvard scientist, Keith Wallace, spoke. According to Wallace, Transcendental Meditation could reduce blood pressure and bring other physical benefits. Jerry Jarvis, head of the Student International Meditation Society (SIMS) told of other benefits of T.M. and of plans for a worldwide campaign to spread the good news of its potential contributions to mankind.

Why are Wallace, Jerry Jarvis, and others so ecstatic about T.M.? Is it because it offers an easy, uncomplicated solution to seemingly insurmountable problems? Is it because it makes few demands upon a person such as a change of moral values or dedication of life and material wealth?

HISTORICAL BACKGROUND AND DEVELOPMENT OF T.M.

It will be helpful to look at the historical background and development of Transcendental Meditation. Maharishi Mahesh Yogi recounts in his writings several revivals of the true understanding of life and the way to fulfillment in history. The first occurred over twenty-five hundred years ago and is recorded in the *Upanishads,* ancient Hindu writings. The second was recorded in the *Bhagavad Gita,* near the time of the Christian era. The second revival was brought by lord Krishna who gave the teaching to Arjuna, the greatest warrior of the age.

Soon the teachings were lost again. Then Shankara, about thirteen hundred years ago, revived the true teaching in its pure state once again. Shankara, the great teacher of the seventh century A.D., was a commentator on the Hindu *Upanishads* and the *Bhagavad Gita.* Shankara established four seats of learning in India to keep this teaching in a pure state and to insure propagation of it. However, his message was also lost after some centuries of purity.[18]

Guru Dev and Maharishi Mahesh Yogi. Maharishi then suggests that there was a vacuum of the pure Vedic and Vedanta teachings until this age. Then Swami Brahmananda Saraswati (called Guru Dev or Divine Teacher) came on the scene and offered the results of his search for God. Maharishi states that he is seeking ways to carry out Guru Dev's desire for world enlightenment. Maharishi started the worldwide Spiritual Regeneration Movement five years after Guru Dev died, in 1958.

Maharishi Mahesh Yogi is now one of the most famous Hindu gurus. He was born in North Central India in 1918. By birth he was a member of the Kshatriya (warrior) caste. His education included a major in physics at Allahabad University, where he graduated at the age of thirty-one. He followed this study with approximately five years of work in a factory. During this time he studied the ancient Vedas, which are the holy books that form the foundation for Hinduism. He also practiced some Yoga. In 1940 Maharishi went into the Himalayan foothills for thirteen years, where he meditated and studied as a disciple of Swami Brahmananda Saraswati. As we have already noted, Guru Dev was a leader of the Shankara tradition of Vedantic Hinduism. Mahesh soon became one of Guru Dev's favorite disciples. He learned Yoga techniques which he was later to simplify.

When Guru Dev died, Mahesh retired to some Himalayan caves to meditate. Two years later he came down from the mountains as a proclaimed master. He gave himself the title of Maharishi (Great Sage), Mahesh (family name), Yogi (a person who has achieved union with god). His reception in India was not outstanding since India is oversupplied with spiritual masters. So he decided to bring his message to the West.[19]

T.M. comes to the United States and the world. Following the "Congress of Spiritual Luminaries" which he addressed in honor of Guru Dev's eighty-ninth birthday anniversary, Maharishi left Madras, India, on the first of more than twelve world tours. He ended up in Hawaii in the early spring of 1959. He stayed there two months and then came to San Francisco in April. By the summertime of 1959 the Spiritual Regeneration Movement was established in Los Angeles. This was the lone T.M. organization until 1965, when student interest prompted the formation of the Student International Meditation Society (SIMS). The movement has now gone from professional people and businessmen to students, both high school and college. The International Meditation Society was later established in the United States to offer courses to the general public. When business and industry became increasingly interested in the creative factor of the T.M. movement, the American Foundation for the

Science of Creative Intelligence was formed.[20]

In 1967 the Beatle's George Harrison, as a by-product of his study of Indian music, investigated Maharishi's ideas and convinced many of his fellow musicians of the merits of Maharishi's teachings. The Beatles, along with Mia Farrow and other celebrities, spread Maharishi's popularity like wildfire. For a period of time the guru enjoyed the international limelight. Soon his popularity sagged. Moving back to India in 1970, Maharishi went back to thé drawing board. He developed a world plan and came back to the West and to the organizations that had been previously established, stronger than before.

The fifth and final branch of the T.M. organization, Maharishi International University, was founded in 1971 on the campus of defunct Parsons College in Iowa. Its avowed purpose is to train teachers and develop curricula and teaching materials for courses in the Science of Creative Intelligence.

The Maharishi has created an ever growing, worldwide organization in the last few years. Since his first visit to the United States in 1959 his organization has trained more than six hundred thousand persons in T.M. in this country alone. Currently more than thirty thousand new meditators are initiated monthly at over three hundred strategically located centers in the United States by more than six thousand teachers. Canada and Western Europe are also reporting increasing numbers of adherents. There are T.M. centers in eighty-nine countries.

Campus chapters of the Student International Meditation Society have active programs on more than one hundred United States college campuses. T.M. centers, retreats, and hotels are busy. Television stations are being purchased.

According to his published world plan, Maharishi hopes to establish 3500 teacher-training centers for 3.5 million teachers in order to reach the world's approximately 3.5 billion people. Eventually the Maharishi expects to teach most meditators by means of television, and to that end he has established the Veda-Vision Engineering Company. This is a division of a larger company in Oakland, California, which is trying to develop an inexpensive line of video equipment.[21]

The Maharishi claims that if only 1 percent of a community or country meditates, the other 99 percent will feel the effects. If 5 percent meditate, great things will happen. Through the practice of T.M. the age of enlightenment is coming, according to the Maharishi.

In order to be one of those 3.5 million teachers who will bring enlightenment, a person must take a twelve-week course at an average cost of over one thousand dollars. The Maharishi himself is the instructor of many of these courses at his revamped resort spa in the Swiss village of Seelisburg. Encouragement is also given to take the Maharishi's advanced course, which comprises thirty-three, two-hour videotaped sessions.

Although the technique is not supposed to be communicated through reading, the T.M. centers do encourage the reading of some of the Maharishi's works for more advancement in the practice of T.M. The books suggested include: *Transcendental Meditation: Serenity Without Drugs* (formerly *The Science of Being and the Art of Living*, 1966); *On the Bhagavad-Gita*, A New Translation and Commentary, 1967; and *Love and God*, 1965.

Selling T.M. to the United States. It is an interesting fact that, although the teaching of T.M. is well established in over eighty-nine countries, it is expanding most rapidly in the United States.

One of the biggest steps to promote T.M. in the United States was provided for the Maharishi by the Illinois House of Representatives when it voted to advocate the use of T.M. in the educational institutions of Illinois in 1972. It is noteworthy that sessions to train T.M. teachers were financed in 1972 by a grant from the National Institute of Mental Health of the Department of Health, Education, and Welfare.

The success of T.M. is due to a carefully worked out program. In the early days of his American program, Maharishi encountered two obstacles to success. He began as a Hindu holy man, importing Hinduism as a new religion. But he found that many secular Westerners viewed religion with suspicion and boredom. Furthermore, the United States' separation of church and state hindered him from teaching T.M. to the masses through the agencies of government.

Maharishi got around these difficulties in two ways. First, he disguised the religious nature of T.M. to pass by the constitutional safeguards. Second, he presented T.M. on two levels. The "ignorant" general public was presented a picture of a new psychological or scientific technique. The true Hindu religious nature of T.M. (the inner reality) is shared only with the "initiates." [22] A T.M. leader states that the program was presented in nonspiritual terms to gain the attention of people who would have rejected it if the presentation had been put in spiritual terms.

THE PRACTICE OF T.M.

At this point we should remember that T.M. utilizes a variation of one of the Hindu Yoga techniques which we have described. The basic technique of Transcendental Meditation involves a *bija* or seed mantra. The seed mantra is firmly implanted in the mind during an initiation ceremony.

In privacy, the meditator closes his eyes and silently repeats the mantra. The mantra is usually composed of syllables drawn from the Vedas and chosen for the effect of the sound rather than for any meaning. When the individual's mantra becomes refined enough in his own mind, theoretically both sound and thoughts will cease automatically.

It is affirmed that T.M.'s power of positive nonthinking will cause one to experience "pure awareness" which is the source of all creative energy and intelligence. The T.M. methods differ from most other meditation methods because they require no strong or continual concentration or focused effort. If you try hard, you will fail. Meditation, the initiate is told, should never be done just before going to bed or sleep will be difficult.

We have already explained the mantras which Hindu gurus use in meditation. A mantra is a form of words or sounds which is believed to have a magical effect when uttered with intent. Mantras are traditionally held to be revealed by the deities or avatars themselves, whose name vibrations are latent within them. By the mantra a god can be summoned, or at any rate his power can be drawn down, by uttering his particular mantra.

According to the Maharishi, the silent, or psychic, repeating of the mantra in T.M. makes possible entry into new spiritual realms. In these realms contact is made with higher beings (spirits and demons).[23]

Continuing developments in T.M.—Levitation and Invisibility. A new development in T.M. advertisements was unfolded in 1977. The newspaper ads promised free lectures on "the ability to levitate by mere intention." People packed T.M. centers to see demonstrations. No actual levitations (lifting up bodies by psychic force) were offered. Instead, advanced meditators told of their experiences in raising their bodies six feet from the floor. In order to learn this "supernormal" ability, intensive training for ten weeks for a total cost of twenty-five hundred dollars was required.

The new development involving levitation was given to advanced teachers in a special training session in Switzerland. The Maharishi told the teachers that the world's consciousness had been sufficiently raised through T.M. to permit this next step in mind-body integration. Over eight hundred of the nine hundred present reported levitation. Some said they could make themselves invisible. Superstrength and superhearing are claimed. That the mind can control matter is what Hindu Yogis have always taught, say T.M. leaders.[24]

The T.M. Initiation Ceremony. The initiation ceremony is the most important step in learning T.M. A candidate must participate in a formal

24

ceremony if he is to receive the secret Sanskrit word or mantra on which he meditates.

Terri Schultz reports that teachers of T.M. compare mantras to blood types and say that they know which mantra best fits each meditator. Their decisions are apparently based on a one-page questionnaire filled out before initiation, on which is listed education, marital status, and a one-word description of the prospective student's current state of mind. Initiates are told to never repeat their mantras aloud. Vocalizing it brings a person back to grosser states of consciousness and might weaken future meditation. After one has practiced T.M. for a sufficient length of time, local T.M. centers offer advanced instruction.

The initiate is required to bring to the ceremony three fruits (no lemons), a minimum of six flowers, and a clean white handkerchief. It is required that the initiate's system be free of nonprescription drugs for a minimum of fifteen days. If the initiate has seen a psychiatrist more than once a week, he is not allowed to take part, the reason being that therapy causes one to be analytical and reflective, which interferes with the practice of T.M.

Upon arrival for the ceremony shoes are removed and one enters an incense-filled, candlelit room. Kneeling before a picture of Maharishi's dead master, the T.M. initiator begins singing the *puja* or a Vedic hymn of worship. This hymn honors the departed masters of the Shankara tradition of Hinduism. After this singing for ten or fifteen minutes, the initiator will rise and give the initiate his personal Sanskrit mantra. Each person (teacher and initiate) repeats the mantra, then the initiate repeats it in his mind, closing his eyes. If thoughts intrude, a person goes back to the word with the mind. He is told to return for the next three consecutive nights for help in learning to meditate, and then he is on his own. Instructions are given to meditate twice a day for twenty minutes at a time. T.M. is claimed to be simple, natural, and easy—a veritable shortcut to happiness.

Testimonials attract many people. Testimonials about T.M. are numerous. T.M. has been endorsed by leading businessmen, politicians, high ranking Army officials, and government leaders. Famous subscribers or practicers of T.M. include Bill Walton (basketball star), Joe Namath (football quarterback), Samantha Jones (cover girl), the Beatles (who have since dropped out), the Rolling Stones, Mia Farrow, Donovan, and Shirley MacLaine.

Reported research, funded in part by the National Institute of Mental Health, claims to have established that the more T.M. one practices, the less a person desires alcohol, tobacco, and especially hard drugs. Although research is still incomplete, T.M. has been recommended as an alternative to drug abuse by officials of the U.S. Bureau of Prisons and the United States Army.

Robert Keith Wallace, now president of the Maharishi International University, published his UCLA doctoral thesis on the relation of T.M. to human physiology. Wallace, a meditator himself, measured various physiological responses to meditation, including changes in oxygen consumption, brain waves, and skin resistance. He observed increases in alpha and theta waves during meditation, particularly in the frontal areas of the brain, and yet the meditators' brain waves kept responding to auditory and light stimuli. The alpha waves were more intense during T.M. than when his subjects merely closed their eyes. The occasional theta waves resembled those of drowsiness or the early stages of sleep.[25]

It is noteworthy that Herbert Benson of Harvard Medical School has modified his earlier commendation of T.M. which he issued in conjunction with Wallace. For Benson, T.M. has no monopoly. Secular techniques like autogenic training and progressive relaxation are equally valid. Religious techniques from Christianity and other groups can also provide what Benson calls the "Relaxation Response."

IS T.M. A RELIGION?

At public T.M. lectures, one is told that T.M. is not a religion. Organizations promoting it are listed as nonprofit *educational* organizations. Official literature adamantly states that T.M. is not another religion. As we have seen, one reason for this emphasis is to keep separate the ideas of religion and the state. The Maharishi sees the United States government as a primary tool to advance his cause, and he wants to avoid American laws, preventing the government from aiding religion. At any rate, regardless of what T.M. advocates say, as indicated above, what comes out in practice is certainly not related to the Hindu religion. A Westerner who does not see this is naive and uncritical. While belief is not *prescribed*, Hindu religious beliefs are taught. The process of interpreting the experience of T.M. to the mediator is based upon a systematic religious philosophy. As we have seen, this philosophy is closely related to the Vedantic Hinduism of Shankara. This truth is being recognized by magazines, like *Psychology Today*, which state that T.M. is clearly a revival of ancient Indian Brahmanism.

In earlier writings and speeches, Maharishi himself stated that T.M. is related to religion. The Maharishi states: "Because none of the scriptures of religion describe or teach T.M., the effectiveness of religions in general has declined worldwide. The true spirit of religion is lacking when it counts only what is right and wrong and creates fear of punishment and hell, and the fear of God in the mind of man. The purpose of religion should be to take away all fear from man." [26] For the Maharishi, the fulfillment of every religion is in the simple practice of transcendental deep meditation. This belongs to the spirit of every religion; it has existed in the early stages of every faith.

According to Maharishi, it is a pity that Christ talked in terms of suffering. The basic premise of every religion should be that man need not suffer in life. No man belonging to any religion should have any place in his life for suffering, tension, immorality, vices, sinful thought, speech, or action. None of these negative aspects of life should exist for a man following religion. A religious life should be a life in bliss, joyfulness, peace, harmony, creativity, and intelligence. [27]

Thus, by his own teaching and philosophical statement, the Maharishi incorporates T.M. into a religion opposed to the basic concepts of Christianity. The suffering of Christ is an essential part of God's redemptive plan for mankind, according to Christianity.

It is well known that the exponents of Transcendental Meditation are attempting to introduce this practice into schools and other public programs under the guise of a religiously neutral form of psychological therapy. Originally billed as the Spiritual Regeneration Movement, it is now presented as a scientific and educational technique or "The Science of Creative Intelligence." We have seen that this is a built-in deception for the uncritical and uninitiated.

The Christian Century magazine featured an article by a Presbyterian pastor in Fairfield, Iowa, the new home of Maharishi International University. Pastor Dilley claims that Transcendental Meditation is not a religion but a technique easily adapted to Christianity. In the same magazine, Professor La More of Iowa Wesleyan College claims that Transcendental Meditation is a religion in secular clothing and could eventually lead a practicer into Hinduism and away from a biblical faith. Its promoters, maintains La More, are violating the American principle of the separation of church and state. [28]

HOW IS THE CHRISTIAN TO EVALUATE T.M.?

The new world promised by many devotees of the Maharishi's technique may sound extremely promising and very appealing. In actual practice it does not come out as promised. The method has serious philosophical and theological flaws that prevent it from being a twentieth-century (substitute) messiah from a Christian perspective.

There is an open and explicit element of worship in the required initiation ceremony. This utilization of the Vedic hymn of worship (puja) would disqualify T.M. as a permissible practice for evangelical Christians in light of the commandment of God (Ex. 20:4-5).

It has also been pointed out that the puja is so constructed in its rhythms and sounds as to produce an altered state of consciousness. In this condition the initiator can transmit the mantra with psychic force at deep levels of the unconscious mind. The mantra, as we have seen, reflects a world view alien to Christianity.

The simplistic nature of T.M. is another weakness that immediately comes to mind. T.M. claims that simply resting the mind and body through meditation brings freedom from confusion, frustration, suffering, and personality problems, all in one swoop.

According to T.M. the answer to every problem is that there is no problem.[29] This easy costless salvation from the day-to-day hang-ups of life is neither realistic nor possible. When held against the torments of grief, loneliness, pain, disease, self-doubt, and anxiety, the Maharishi's talk about "bliss-consciousness" seems romantic and even cheap. This view reflects basic Hindu teachings. A person is to transcend this world of maya (illusion), the world of problem and pain. This is accomplished by attaining higher levels of consciousness where there is no duality, no good and bad, no right and wrong, and no problems and pain.

From a Christian perspective another weakness of T.M. is that it seeks the answer to man's problems from within man himself. The basic precept of the Maharishi is that we can find god *within* us as a spark of the divine. In fact, the Maharishi teaches that Jesus is no more of a god than the great Hindu masters or others who have achieved god-realization.

Peterson suggests that the big drawing card of T.M. for many people is that it requires no repudiation of the past and does not insist on any promises to change in the future. The Beatles liked it because there was no fuss and no bother; it called for no change in their life-styles. From a Christian perspective, T.M. fails to recognize man's biggest problem: sin. According to biblical teaching, man has a sinful heart and the root of his mind does not yield thought bubbles of divine wonder and intention, but wicked devices and selfish ends, all in revolt against the sovereignty of God.[30]

The Maharishi does not give any guidance for morality nor does he give any standard of ethics. The primary requirement is to sink a shaft of light (your mantra) into your mind and then your mind will gravitate to the light to find "absolute bliss." When you gain pure consciousness you automatically perform right action.

There is obviously a great difference between T.M. and Christian prayer. Jesus teaches that Christian prayer is to be intelligent communication between two persons (God and man), not meaningless repetition of the same word over and over (Matt. 6:7–9).

In Christian meditation a person actively uses his mind to study, analyze, and apply the Word of God. In T.M. the senses are withdrawn from external fields of perception. The mind is placed in neutral and ultimately dismissed when cosmic consciousness (samadhi) is experienced.

The Spiritual Counterfeits Project research contends that behind the innocent and seemingly helpful T.M. movement is a disciplined, esoteric organization filled with spiritual pride, moral pragmatism, power drives, and rigid mind controls. Upon probing into the world view of T.M., it becomes clear that it is a thoroughly traditional Hindu world view. This view is filled with political and social attitudes which are elitist and reactionary. The Hindu Vedantist approach to matters of social rehabilitation is virtually nil. The T.M. movement seems to have no outreach projects of any sort beyond the direct expansion of the movement itself.[31]

Lessons to be learned from T.M. Haddon suggests that Christians should use the occasion of the rise of T.M. to ask themselves what they and their churches can do to fill the spiritual vacuum exposed by the invasion of this alien religious system. A generation of young people ignorant of the Bible and of the transforming power of Christ in their own or others' lives has arisen. Creative and authentic means should be found to fill this vacuum with alternative Christian thinking.[32]

The significance of T.M. cannot be defined simply as a countercultural fad. The growing popularity of such a New Consciousness group points up the loss of Christian devotion or understanding in many American circles. Many see the United States as so spiritually starved that Far Eastern New Consciousness groups are finding fertile ground for their teachings.

As has been indicated, the Christian response will surely involve understanding and incarnation of the dynamics and resources of the Christian faith. For informed choices, an in-depth knowledge of the nature and teaching of groups such as Transcendental Meditation should be sought.

4
The Hare Krishna Movement
(International Society for Krishna Consciousness)

In 1965, while I was on sabbatical leave in New York City, publicity was being given to a new religious leader from India, Swami Bhakti Vedanta Prabhupada. Sitting beneath a tree in an East Village park, he chanted the name of the Hindu god, Krishna, to the rhythm of his cymbals. Little did I realize that in less than a dozen years, the most colorful and controversial New Consciousness group in America would develop from his efforts.

While writing this material, I had a call from a distraught mother concerning her son who has joined Hare Krishna, or the International Society for Krishna Consciousness (ISKCON). A recent university graduate, the young man has shaved his head except for a ponytail of long hair. He is wearing a loin cloth and a bright orange robe. On his forehead is a daub of white clay, the mark of Krishna. The mother can see him on the streets of Houston, thumping small drums, ringing bells, and chanting "Hare Krishna."

Why has this affluent, middle-class, young man joined such a far out group? What is this group? What should the mother do? Her minister and psychiatrist offered little information or help. Like this mother, many people are concerned and want to learn about Hare Krishna.

WHY THE INTEREST IN SUCH A RELATIVELY SMALL GROUP? WHY SHOULD WE BE CONCERNED WITH A GROUP LIKE HARE KRISHNA WHICH HAS ONLY TEN THOUSAND FULL-TIME DEVOTEES?

One reason is that it symbolizes in the most dramatic way possible the whole youth revolt in the United States which began in the 1960s. The Hare Krishna group became a vehicle of the protest of American middle-class young people against their former life-styles. Interest in Hare Krishna reminds us once again in an unusual way of the fact that people have emotional and religious cravings and desire fellowship, meaning, and authority. It is one example of how alienation, insecurity, and loss of meaning can be overcome through a shared experience of religious enthusiasm and strict discipline.[33]

Hare Krishna also attracts our interest because it is a vivid example of the religious and emotional nature of some of the New Consciousness groups. The founder of Hare Krishna, Swami Prabhupada, early in his American ministry, offered Krishna consciousness as an alternative to drugs. Four-foot high, multicolored posters on the San Francisco Krishna Temple stated: "Stay High Forever. No more coming down. Turn on. Tune in. Awaken your transcendental nature! End all bring-downs. Swami Bhakti Vedanta has come to this country to spiritually guide young Americans."[34]

Another reason for interest in Hare Krishna is the insight which it gives to some of the weaknesses of America's liberal Christian denominations. It also throws light on some of the reasons for the growth and appeal of the charismatic and conservative Christian groups in recent years in the United States.

THE RELATION OF HARE KRISHNA TO CLASSIC HINDUISM

To properly understand ISKCON, its similarities and differences in relation to classical Hinduism should be noted. As we have seen, the more intellectual Hindu sees Brahman (god or ultimate reality) as impersonal. In Transcendental Meditation we saw that the self is one with god. The goal of Hinduism is to realize this oneness.

The common people of India cling to more concrete conceptions and manifestations of god or Brahman. Popular teachings center upon three great manifestations or gods as objects of worship: Brahma, the creator; Vishnu, the protector; Siva, the destroyer. Brahma is not to be confused with the impersonal Brahman.

Vishnu, the protector, is believed to have come to earth in several forms when world crises required such divine manifestations. Rama, hero of the Hindu epic, the *Ramayana,* is one avatar or incarnation of Vishnu. Lord Krishna, a character in the Hindu classic, the *Bhagavad Gita,* is another. Popular Hinduism worships Rama and Krishna as incarnations of Vishnu.

In a way which more orthodox Hindu groups say is heretical, Hare Krishna inverts the order mentioned above. Krishna is the supreme personality, the lord, the complete whole, and the absolute truth. Brahma, Vishnu, and Siva are seen as expansions or forms of Krishna. Krishna is supreme and unborn. He is the force of the universe and yet lives in the souls of all men. All other gods are Krishna but people don't know it.

Brahma, for example, has only 78 percent of Krishna's attributes. Groups rooted in the Vedanta thought of Shankara, (such as Transcendental Meditation) seek to merge with Brahman. For the ISKCON followers this is to miss the absolute pleasure which is in Krishna.[35]

Unlike Vedanta thought (Transcendental Meditation), there is no final merging of the self into Brahman or god. Rather for ISKCON there is a sportive transcendental love and fellowship with a very personal god, Krishna, in one of his heaven worlds. Thus Hare Krishna is a version of Bhakti Yoga. Devotion is the way of release from the endless rounds of rebirth known as the wheel of samsara. This is in contrast to *Karma Yoga* (good works) and *Jnana Yoga* (knowledge) which are alternative forms of salvation in Hinduism.[36]

Reincarnation, a basic idea of Hinduism, is kept by ISKCON. In fact, Hare Krishna leaders are said to have been prepared for their spiritual destination by previous incarnations.

Advanced Hindu scholars see the stories of the appearances, amorous exploits, and pastimes of Krishna as largely allegories and myths. A character named Krishna perhaps lived, but many of the events about his life described in the *Bhagavad Gita* were allegorical. Instead of 3000 B.C. these scholars suggest that Krishna probably lived near the time of Christ.

Hare Krishnas, however, preach a literal interpretation of every reported story about Krishna. He walked the earth five thousand years ago in India. He danced with a hundred women at a time giving each one orgiastic bliss. Krishna had a long love affair with the girl Radha. In addition to being literal, these stories are said to symbolize the relation of god and man now and in the future.[37]

THE FOUNDING AND DEVELOPMENT OF HARE KRISHNA

Beginnings with Chaitanya. The roots of the modern Hare Krishna movement go back to a Hindu religious leader, Chaitanya Mahaprabha. Born in 1486, he was initiated as a Vishnuite at the age of sixteen. Soon he began dancing and chanting the name of Krishna in the streets of the city.[38]

As was mentioned earlier, one of the Hindu ways of salvation is through bhakti or devotion to an avatar of god. Chaitanya taught this bhakti way. For him, direct love of lord Krishna was the way to burn off ignorance, overcome bad karma (or retribution), and attain bliss. Orthodox Hindus denounced him for worshiping exclusively by dancing, chanting, and singing Krishna's name.

Since 1500 A.D., Chaitanya's sect of Krishnaism has continued in India. The sect has come to say that Chaitanya was an appearance of Krishna to revive the true worship of Krishna. Since 1500 an unbroken chain of succession has come down to the leader and founder of the American group, Swami Prabhupada, who died in 1977.

Revival by Prabhupada. Born in 1896, Prabhupada studied at the University of Calcutta. He had a successful career with a pharmaceutical firm. During his thirties he became interested in religion. He was initiated into the Vishnava or Vishnuite sect in 1933 by Swami Saraswati. Shortly before Saraswati's death, he passed the mantle of leadership to Prabhupada and ordered him to take the message of Chaitanya to the West.[39]

Prabhupada continued as a spiritual leader and businessman in India until 1965. He began publishing the English magazine *Back to Godhead* in 1944. He was given the title "Bhakti Vedanta," meaning "devotional knowledge," for his work. Finally at the age of 58, in 1959, he renounced his wife and five children, abandoned his business, and put on the robes of a Hindu monk. He began full-time study with Siddhartha Goswami. From then on he was called "Swami." In India, which is a land of many sects, the Krishna group never became a major religious force.

Sensational development in America. In 1965 the swami set out for the United States with a steamship ticket provided by a wealthy Hindu woman. He is said to have arrived in the United States with only five dollars and a small box of Hindu scriptures. This same Swami Prabhupada, less than ten years later, could be seen in a chauffered Mercedes, with police escort, driving into San Francisco Golden Gate Park for a Hare Krishna celebration. More than ten thousand were in attendance.[40] By this time his movement had become worldwide with more than ten thousand full-time devotees and many more part-time adherents. In contrast, I well remember the small group that he first attracted in New York's East Side.

His personal attraction to many youth was little short of sensational. Poet Alan Ginsberg eulogized Krishna consciousness in poetry and Beatle George Harrison declared its virtues in song. *The Village Voice* also began to publicize the movement. It is not surprising that as early as 1968 many of his followers were saying that, like Chaitanya, Swami Prabhupada was the incarnation of god or Krishna for our era.

THE DISTINCTIVE TEACHINGS OF HARE KRISHNA

Although the followers of ISKCON say that Krishna consciousness is incomprehensible to the intellect, the movement does have an agreed upon theology.

1. Krishna is recognized as the highest personality of the godhead. Devotion and love of him will bring Krishna consciousness or bliss.

2. Since Krishna is so far removed, a spiritual master is needed. He

must be within the line of "disciplic succession" that goes back to Chaitanya. Swami Prabhupada is appointed to be god's representative for our time in distributing the love of god. He is called "His Divine Grace." He is higher than Christ. He has the powers and prerogatives of god himself. Devotees should surrender completely to him as their guru.

3. Man has a spiritual nature like Krishna. The soul is individual and at the same time part of the divine soul. But man also has a material body made of lower energy. Man's body and the material world are maya or illusion. The material world is superficial and unreal. Advertising, supermarkets, movies, and newspapers are all senseless diversions. As indicated, man should concentrate on the fact that he is a spirit-soul. Man should say, "I am not this body." Man should wage war against the body.

4. In order to be delivered from the illusory material world, one must develop Krishna consciousness. Certain techniques can help a devotee to be completely aware of Krishna with all the senses.

a) Chanting the mantra is the basic ritual of the ISKCON liturgy. The mantra consists of the Sanskrit words: Hare Krishna, Hare Krishna, Krishna, Krishna, Hare, Hare, Hare Rama, Hare Rama, Rama, Rama, Hare, Hare. *Hare* is the vocative form of the word for the energies of god. Krishna is the name of the supreme lord. Rama is an earlier divine descent of Krishna. Chanting attunes the devotee to the supreme energy of Krishna. This chant, sung to the accompaniment of drums, cymbals, and tamborines also revives man's original pure consciousness. The instruments provide "transcendental sound vibrations." Man's ignorance and karma are burned away.

Each devotee is expected to chant the mantra at least sixteen rounds each day. A round consists of singing the mantra once on each of 108 prayer beads. By using the beads the devotee is remembering Krishna with his touch.[41]

Critics point out that chanting is a form of psychological conditioning. In repeating the mantra, the external world is shut out.

b) Eating is also a religious act. Meals are called prasadam or love feasts. Only two "yoga diet" meals are eaten a day. The protein items are mostly dried bean mush and raw chick peas. No meat, fish, or eggs are allowed. The food is offered to lord Krishna in a religious ritual before it is eaten. Eating the food is an act of devotion, an aid to god-consciousness, and a way of remembering Krishna through the sense of taste. It is believed that Krishna's energy floods the body of the devotee when the food is digested.[42]

c) Another ritual act is worshiping and attending to the needs of several deity statues. These idols are given food, incense, and flowers. In a ceremony the deities are symbolically bathed and dressed. Such an act recalls Krishna's memory through sight. A divine bush is also worshiped.[43]

d) Krishna is also remembered through the smell of incense and flowers. ISKCON owns a lucrative incense business called Spiritual Sky. Devotees believe that Krishna is physically present in the aromatic fragrances.

HARE KRISHNA LIFE-STYLE

As already indicated, Hare Krishna calls for a radical change in life-style. On entering ISKCON, all facets of the convert's prior identity are surrendered.

The hair of the male is shaved. The hair is said to be for the sole purpose of sexual attraction. A shiny scalp is seen as submission to Krishna. Only a pigtail is left on the back of the head. Krishna will use this to pull the devotee into heaven. All personal effects are given to the temple. A new Sanskrit name is assigned. Orange or yellow Hindu robes are supplied and worn at all times. Sex (outside of marriage), meat, gambling, alcohol, cigarettes, and drugs are forbidden. Since most members come from prosperous homes, the life of poverty and ascetic denial is especially dramatic. Comfort is no consideration. "You are not this body" is a teaching to be remembered.[44]

A pre-initiation stage usually lasts at least six months. The initiation, fire ceremony or holy name ritual, is quite elaborate. During the ceremony the Sanskrit name and three strands of neck beads are awarded. The beads are to be worn until the devotee dies! The 108 beads are similar to Catholic rosary beads. They represent the 108 cowherd lovers of Krishna. Each must be chanted upon with the sixteen-word "great mantra."

After another six months or so from the initiation date, the devotee is eligible for initiation as a brahmin. At this service men receive a sacred thread to be worn over the chest. At this time, a secret mantra, to be chanted three times a day, is given to both men and women.

The next highest stage is sannyasi. This stage is only for especially devoted men. Few reach such a holy stage. Devotees prostrate on the floor in the presence of a sannyasi.

Despite a strict rule of celibacy outside of marriage, some of Hare Krishna's worship materials are sensual. In meditation, for example, the devotee seeks to visualize the love engagements that Krishna carried on with a hundred women at one time. Hare Krishna ideology thus denies sexuality and at the same time tantalizes the devotee with tales and images of a sexy god.[45]

Celibacy is encouraged but marriage is allowed. If married, couples may have sexual intercourse once a month. This can only happen on a night designated in the Vedas for fertility. The sexual act is allowed only after the couple has chanted for five or six hours, doing fifty rounds on their japa beads in order to purify themselves. Sex is strictly for procreation. It is not to be used for the enjoyment of the senses or to establish closeness to a mate.[46]

The daily schedule for the full-time devotee is based on a pattern that comes from India. All senses are to be engaged in the service of Krishna. To this end, each hour is carefully planned.

The schedule begins at 3:00 or 3:45 A.M. It is mostly composed of chants and prayers until 9:30 or 10:00 A.M. Next comes two hours on the street for chanting and selling. In the afternoon there is more street work. In the evening study and chanting continue until 9:15. Retirement is at 10:00 P.M. Six hours is the maximum sleep allowed.

Little mention is made of specific moral duties in Hare Krishna circles since a moral life is thought to follow devotion to Krishna. The religious transformation of man's consciousness will bring in the new age. The transformation is to be a psychological one rather than through changed institutions. Someday, Krishnas claim, there will be only one political party: people will not vote but chant. Social problems will automatically disappear since people will be unified by Krishna consciousness.[47]

True or Vedic knowledge is transcendental and spiritual and cannot be understood by educational procedures. Study of such spiritual knowledge will only take you so far. In order to truly understand it, you must practice it. It is something you know when you feel it.

Formal secular education is rejected. Schooling is held but it is profoundly different from traditional education! Spiritual knowledge is unified and grounded in personal experience. The end of learning is self-realization.[48]

THE ORGANIZATION OF HARE KRISHNA

The temple president has absolute authority and answers to the successor of Swami Prabhupada. Practical and spiritual procedures are carefully followed. Even marriages are allowed or refused by the temple president.

There are forty temples in the United States and Canada and a hundred more throughout the world. Not all people who attend the temple are full-time followers. Some follow secular pursuits, attend temple ceremonies, and contribute money to Krishna.

A basic activity of most devotees is chanting and singing on the sidewalks and in such places as airports. Some followers chant and dance while others sell *Back to Godhead* magazines and ask for donations. Wigs, sport shirts, and slacks are now allowed in order to camouflage members in some areas. Sometimes members dress up like Santa Claus. In certain cases, people are told by the devotees that they are feeding people in India in order to raise money. Such techniques supplement sales work. Each devotee who sells in the United States is said to bring in from sixty to one hundred dollars a day. In Germany, the average for each seller is said to be over two hundred dollars a day. The money is turned over to the temple leaders.

Members are taught that the Krishna literature will help save souls for Krishna. Devotees often accost clients in a vigorous way in airports and shopping malls and on the streets.

Incense called Spiritual Sky is also manufactured and sold. On the back of the incense package are directions to send for information on "mind expansion." This, of course, is information about Hare Krishna. People are also invited by the street workers to free Indian banquets with music and dance. At these Sunday evening dinners Hare Krishna speakers urge their prospects to leave behind a life of "lust and intoxication" to follow the true life of love for Krishna.

THE RELATION OF HARE KRISHNA TO MIND CONTROL AND DEPROGRAMMING

Former members of Hare Krishna report that the techniques used in ISKCON study and worship constitute a form of mind control. One girl reported that the devotees chanting japa silently and listening to lectures reminded her of Orwell's novel *1984.* In the Philadelphia temple Prabhupada's lectures have been played over the loudspeaker system twenty-four hours a day.

Starchy, low protein diets combined with limited sleep wear down physical and psychological defenses and make indoctrination and suggestibility much easier.

A young man from Cincinnati reports, "They took away my will to think. To advance in the Hare Krishna order, more and more chanting was required. You kept hypnotizing yourself by chanting." Chanting also provides a structured expression of emotions normally reserved for intimate relationships.[49]

Receiving a new name in the initiation ceremony reinforces the act of severing all family and cultural ties. The Hare Krishna initiation service inaugurates a process which often results in changes of voice, posture,

37

mannerisms, and even handwriting. These changes reflect a shift in personality and world view. All parents and friends in the world are to be seen as merely "flesh relationships," outsiders or karmis. Critical parents are seen as demons.

The entire life structure of the Hare Krishna order serves to deindividualize personal relationships. The shaving of the hair is an important initial event in deindividualizing and symbolically desexualizing the recruit. Mirrors are not provided in Krishna temples. The human body is seen as an obstacle to self-realization. Consequently, devotees have little regard for their bodies and appearance.

It is difficult to talk to Hare Krishna devotees. They are told not to waste time in intellectual discussions. Knowledge of Krishna alone is meaningful. And this knowledge is primarily to be lived and experienced rather than discussed. Discussion is even seen as a hindrance to the development of Krishna consciousness.[50]

In the light of such mind-control techniques, it is not surprising that some parents go to extreme measures such as kidnapping and deprogramming to rescue their children from the Hare Krishna movement. Some cases get to the courts and raise a very difficult and delicate problem of religious liberty and religious freedom versus mind control.

A recent case in New York state related to Hare Krishna was aired in the national media. It brought forth extensive discussion. The prosecutor accused the Hare Krishnas of unlawful imprisonment of a twenty-four-year-old college girl on the theory that she had lost her free will due to Hare Krishna mind control. The prosecutor told the New York *Times* that the Hare Krishnas are "creating an army of zombies and robots who could undermine the government." The defense attorney and the American Civil Liberties Union stated that the case is a "classic freedom of religion issue." Harvard theologian Harvey Cox made the comment, "Some Oriental religious movements bother us because they pose a threat to the values of career success, individual competition, personal ambition, and consumption on which our economic system depends. We forget that Christianity, taken literally, could cause similar disquietude." [51]

The New York Supreme Court Justice before whom the case was tried dismissed the case as a "direct and blatant violation" of constitutionally guaranteed religious freedom. The judge stated that the Hare Krishnas' "indoctrination and constant chanting" may create "an inability to think, to be reasonable or logical," but that does not make it any less a religion. Furthermore, the young woman voluntarily submitted to the tightly regulated life in the local temple. No physical coercion was used. The judge said that he sympathized with the "hurt, fear, and loneliness" of parents when children reject their former life, but, he added, the law sees nothing wrong with "unconventional" belief, proselytizing, chanting, or self-denial.[52]

After a study of other representative New Consciousness groups and their techniques, we will undertake a further discussion of freedom of choice, mind control, and deprogramming.

INSIGHTS FROM HARE KRISHNA HELPFUL IN UNDERSTANDING CHARISMATIC AND CONSERVATIVE CHRISTIANS

Religious devotion to Krishna and religious experience are all-important to Hare Krishna devotees. As a result, the Krishna people accept literally all the stories of the appearances and pastimes of Krishna. The words of scriptures such as the *Bhagavad Gita* are to be accepted just as they are, literally. The religious texts exist primarily to support their devotion to Krishna. The Krishna devotee also wants to keep the precepts of belief the same way as they were originally taught by Krishna himself.[53]

There is a similar approach found among some charismatic and conservative Christians. In majoring on religious experience with Jesus as central and crucial and meaningful, the scriptural accounts are not questioned. After having the experience of glossolalia (speaking in tongues) both conservative and some so-called liberal Christians often state that biblical criticism or biblical background study are no longer important to them. The Bible is now meaningful just as it is written. These Christians see through the eyes of faith, with a vision originating in a mystical experience with Christ. The objective world of logic and analysis has lost interest for them.[54]

HARE KRISHNA AND SECULAR CRITICS

Strong denunciation of Hare Krishna has come from the feminist movement. They are outraged by the inferior and degrading status of women in Hare Krishna society. The marriage policies and attitudes toward sex are also criticized.

ISKCON women are discouraged from doing anything on their own. If they go out on errands, they are always accompanied by other ISKCON members. The married woman is to be completely submissive and a constant servant to her husband. There is strict sex segregation in the temple.

It is also pointed out by Krishna critics that the Hare Krishnas have done little to feed or care for the poor in India or elsewhere.[55]

It has already been indicated that the views of Hare Krishna are quite contrary to evangelical Christianity. Krishna's bliss consciousness is quite different from Christian salvation. For the Christian, man's problems are not primarily rooted in ignorance and illusion but in sin and rebellion against God's plan and purpose for man. For help, man sees the unique life, death, and resurrection of Jesus Christ as the only sufficient answer.[56]

If everything in this world is mere illusion, then the concepts of good and evil fall into that category. Hence, suffering of all kinds, wars, and injustice are seen as a passing unreality.

There are many lessons, however, that can be learned by the Christian community from a study of the Hare Krishna movement. Many of the young people in ISKCON once belonged to one of the established Christian denominations. Some report that the transcendental and experiential elements were lacking in their Christian backgrounds. Christian groups who will meet young people's needs should find a place for religious experience and the vertical dimension in their proclamation of the Christian message.

There are other inherent but often neglected doctrines in Christianity which are seen as important in the light of Hare Krishna success. These doctrines include need for fellowship, religious discipline and hardship, and authority.

Inherent also in Christianity are two emphases which should mean much to those who are tempted to be drawn to Hare Krishna. One is the centrality of the death of Christ as an expression of God's love for needy men. Man's past and continued sins can be resolved and dealt with in a proper appropriation of Christ's vicarious death. The other doctrine is the power of the risen Christ and the Holy Spirit for a continuing life of spiritual happiness and victory.

5
Tantric Hinduism and Kundalini

In a course on "Mysticism and the Occult" which I was teaching at Rice University, a brilliant premedical student suggested that he was investigating one of the world's most powerful New Consciousness groups. He was referring to Tantric Hinduism and Kundalini. Tantra, as it is sometimes called, also has a Buddhist version. The student's class presentation involving Kundalini body charts pointed out that this ancient religious consciousness technique is attracting widespread interest in the United States. It was also noted that Tantric Hinduism is very powerful but potentially dangerous.

In recent years a prominent advertising executive from Iowa, Gene Kieffer, has founded the Kundalini Research Foundation to promote the acceleration of human consciousness through Tantra and Kundalini. Kieffer is especially interested in promoting the view of Gopi Krishna, a contemporary Hindu Kundalini expert.[57]

Scholars such as W. Edward Mann suggest that Wilhelm Reich's controversial theory of life energy is a secular counterpart of some Tantra ideas.[58] Carl Jung, the eminent psychiatrist, has been attracted to many of the techniques of Tantra, such as the use of the mandala.

Tantra and contemporary interest in sexuality. One facet of Tantra's emphasis is the importance of the body and sexuality in attaining higher consciousness. This renewed interest coincides with an unusual resurgence of books and studies on sexuality in conservative Christian circles. Marabel Morgan's *Total Woman* and *Total Joy* have been national best sellers. Conservative religious publishing houses are issuing books such as *Solomon on Sex*. Masters and Johnson, eminent sexologists, have recently employed a prominent conservative pastor as their theological advisor. This former pastor plans to go to conservative theological seminaries to promote a more adequate and realistic sexual perspective.

Hindu Tantra advocates maintain that right-hand Tantraism (as opposed to the more sensual left-hand group) can furnish a constructive approach to sexuality. According to these Tantric advocates, some conservative Christian approaches, such as that of *Total Woman*, reflect male

41

chauvinism. Much secular discussion, such as the *Playboy* philosophy, reduces women to little more than "play things."

The Tantra advocates see in their approach the opportunity to view sexuality in the perspective of heightened religious consciousness. The ideal is to see masculinity and femininity as complementary rhythms calling for a deeper integration. Ritual exercises taught in Hindu Tantraism call for a more authentic communion between two caring individuals. In this approach a woman finds her personhood enhanced rather than depleted. All sexual relationships are to be gathered up into a religious perspective.[59]

THE HINDU BACKGROUND OF TANTRA

In our discussion of Transcendental Meditation, Shankara Vedanta Hinduism was seen as the basic underlying view. Brahman (impersonal god) alone exists. All else is maya. Transcendental Meditation, through an inward repetition of a mantra or sacred word, seeks to sink the soul or self back into god. Hare Krishna uses the chant to extract its followers from the subtle web of illusion spun by sense experience. As we have seen, Hare Krishna practices a rigid asceticism.

Trantric Hinduism shifts emphasis. Developing in the third and fourth centuries A.D., it advocated a practical, experimental, earthy approach rather than a philosophical and ascetic one. It ridiculed the Hindus who concerned themselves with asceticism, clothes, and diet. Tantra strongly affirms the body and its significance for religious understanding.[60]

Tantraism utilizes a complex and mysterious set of spiritual attitudes and practices. It is a road of enlightenment which employs powerful initiations, shock therapy techniques, magical-seeming arts and chants as well as sexual imagery and ritual. It uses imagination instead of repressing it. The techniques listed are used to induce consciousness-changing experiences.[61]

The methods of Tantra were secret for many centuries. Even today the inner meaning of the methods used is transmitted orally from guru to student. Since sexual imagery is employed, it is often misused. Left-hand Tantra is the designation for those who exploit a sexual and physical interpretation.[62]

As we have already seen, Hindu religious teachings appear in many different forms. For the more educated, god, for example, is presented as an abstract impersonal principle known as Brahman. For the popular mind, Brahman, the impersonal absolute, is revealed as Brahma (the creator), Vishnu (the protector), and Siva (the destroyer or transformer). Each god has a female counterpart or consort.

For some groups, Siva is regarded as the highest god, manifesting both creative and destructive energy. His female counterpart or consort is Shakti, who is also known as Kali or Parvati. In contrast to Siva, the creative principle of the world is expressed through Shakti. This eternal mother offers a focus for vivid and emotional worship.

METHODS OF TANTRA (TOOLS OF TRANSFORMATION)

The novice is initiated into the practice of a particular Tantric path by a guru. The follower seeks identity with Siva and Shakti (Kali) through different methods.

1. The use of yantras and mandalas. These are geometrical and circular diagrams for holding attention during meditation. They are visible diagrams of the god's powers.

2. The use of mantras or sounds which induce a definite state of consciousness.

KUNDALINI (RAISING THE SERPENT POWER)

The most dramatic aspect of Tantra is the so-called raising of the serpent power, or kundalini. Kundalini teaches that a potent nucleus of vital energy, a repository of physical and sexual power, dwells at the base of the spine. Kundalini is visualized by Hindu Tantrists as a small serpent lying in a spiral of three and one-half coils at the base of the spine. Through certain Yogic techniques this power can be awakened and aroused and drawn up the spinal column.[63]

These Kundalini techniques to draw the power up the spinal column include many of the major techniques of Yoga. Awakening the Kundalini calls for bodily posture, hand gestures (mudra), mystic syllables (mantra), breath control, eye focusing, symbolic diagrams (yantra), and super-concentration. Breath control is especially important.[64]

Opening of the chakras or energy centers. In the process of moving the Kundalini up the spine, certain chakras are opened. The chakras are seen as lotus centers of dormant psychic energy. They are further described as psychic dynamos or centers of superphysical energy. They have no physiological existence and cannot be laid out on a dissecting table. They can only be known through mediation experience. The chakras are similar to the Chinese pressure points which are pricked in acupuncture. The chakras are part of the Hindu concept of man's "subtle body."

The chakras are located along the spinal column at such places as the base of the spine, the region of the sex organs, the heart, the neck, above the eyebrows, and just above the crown of the head. They are arranged along a shaft of the subtle body called the Rod of Brahma.

According to Tantra advocates, the Kundalini lies asleep in the average person. This is good. If disturbed or ignorantly raised, the Kundalini will cause an abnormal arousal of the baser instincts and passions. To seek to raise the Kundalini or open the chakras apart from a spiritual purpose is both pointless and hazardous.

A proper raising of the Kundalini is said to produce remarkable states of awareness. The first awareness of Kundalini's awakening is a sensation of warmth which grows from warmth to a burning heat. Each chakra pierced and opened brings a new experience, new power, and a new vision. Oftentimes strange sounds are heard.[65]

The final bliss of Kundalini raising. The final objective of Kundalini raising may take many years. It is achieved when the Kundalini or serpent power reaches the final chakra point inside the skull. With a psychic explosion it is said to awaken a ten-thousand-petal lotus. This is a graphic way of describing complete cosmic consciousness and god-realization. Descriptions are vivid. Brilliant stars and flaming tongues are seen. A realized person sees an entire world inside of his head complete with its own miniature mountain, lake, sun, and moon. In the midst of this world, the god Siva is seen enthroned. This is union, absorption, identity. The transcendent state of being-consciousness-bliss has been reached.[66]

Sexual union and Kundalini. Raising the Kundalini or serpent power using Yogic techniques is often described apart from any symbolic or actual sexual imagery. If sexual materials are used in right-hand Tantra, ritual sexual union (Maithuna) is seen as a sacred ceremony. The entire ritual involves twelve months before physical sexual union is experienced. The rites are practiced by stages.[67]

Sexuality is important to Tantraism because it is a tremendous evoker of energy. The skilled guru leads the persons involved to sublimate the sexual energy to the spiritual quest.

Sexuality is also a symbol and sacrament of the Hindu view of reality. The male Tantrist identifies himself with the male deity, Siva, the absolute. The female partner identifies with Siva's consort, Shakti, who is the phenomenal or actual universe. When the couple, at the end of the ritual, unite, they mystically unite the absolute and the universe in a flash of ecstasy.

Some Tantrists see the male surrendering his energy to the goddess whom he regards as incarnate within his female partner. The rite consequently symbolizes the manner in which the phenomenal or actual world is maintained.

In the sexual rites one can see the potential danger of Tantra. The left-hand group takes a more physical approach. The right-hand or more

44

spiritual Tantra group warns that if self has not been negated and identified with the god, the ritual sex act becomes merely lust and not participation in divine mysteries.[68]

The more conservative Hindu Tantric groups regard all sexual references in Tantric ritual literature as strictly symbolic. The male worshiper's contact with the female partner is strictly mental.[69]

EVANGELICAL CHRISTIANITY, SEXUALITY, AND KUNDALINI

Biblical groups have traditionally had difficulty in dealing with the dynamics of sexuality and femininity. To use Chinese terms, the West, under the influence of the biblical tradition, has expressed yang or the male force most strongly. Our God is Jehovah, our Father in heaven. There has been a patriarchal emphasis.

The Far East, in contrast, has expressed yin or the female emphasis. It has emphasized the mother principle.[70] Many see the current interest in the Far East as an interest provoked by an attempt to restore a missing female emphasis to the West.

Christians respond to such discussions by emphasizing the basic Hebrew emphasis on the goodness of the body. Jesus, as God's Son, was incarnated in a body. Jesus displayed both masculine and feminine qualities. He taught that God was both holy and love. Holiness has traditionally been associated with the male and love with the female. Women were some of Jesus' earliest and most loyal followers. In a first-century world that seemed to either worship or despise the body, Jesus neutralized the body and sex. They are inherently neither good nor evil. The important thing is how they are used.

The church is described in the New Testament as the bride of Christ. The Holy Spirit is known as being tender and intimate in his appeal. In the midst of a patriarchal society, the apostle Paul wrote to the Galatians that, "In Christ there is neither male nor female." Some of Paul's earliest and most ardent followers were women.

Despite its inherent affirmative attitude toward the body and sexuality, the evangelical Christian tradition can learn from Tantric Hinduism. Facing such a challenge, it should restudy its own background and find there resources for a balanced view of the human body and sexuality.

6

The Sai Baba Movement

An example of the extreme approaches of some Hindu gurus is seen in the life and alleged miracles of Satya Sai Baba. The Sai Baba movement continues to grow in the United States.

Born in 1926, Sai Baba announced in 1963 that he was an avatar, or divine incarnation of Krishna and of Siva and Shakti, (Siva's) consort. Sai Baba's unique emphasis is his claim to perform miracles. His followers say he cures diseases by a wave of his hand. He is said to materialize out of his body an aromatic gray ash, called vibhuti. At certain festivals, he is said to produce from his mouth one or two small, oblong pieces of stone called linga. The linga is a symbol of Siva.[71]

Sai Baba has never been to the United States but says that a visit is unnecessary. He claims that he can communicate with his followers by telepathy and bring them god-realization in this way. Followers say that his astral body, accompanied by the odor of special incense, calls on disciples who need help anywhere in the world.[72]

Satya Sai Baba, to use his full name, has the biggest following of any guru in India and his influence is spreading in the United States.[73] Indian weekly magazines are filled with reports and controversies about the pudgy, frizzy-haired guru. One magazine headline asks, "Challenge to Sai Baba—is he God?" Another magazine proclaims, "God is an Indian." Sai Baba himself states, "In my present avatar I have come armed with the fullness of the power of the formless God to save humanity."

Sai Baba's headquarters, called the Haven of Supreme Bliss, is fast assuming the status and symbol of a Hindu vatican. There are Hindu dissenters, such as the vice-chancellor of Bangalore University, who claim Sai Baba is little more than a popular magician.

In America, his representative is Indra Devi. The wife of a German doctor, Indra heads a growing American Sai Baba movement.[74]

7
Baba Ram Dass and Bubba Free John

Since the 1960s America has been besieged by United States-born gurus. Two of the most colorful persons who can be seen as symbolic of many others are Baba Ram Dass and Bubba Free John.

BABA RAM DASS (RICHARD ALPERT)

In attendance at a psychic fair, I went into a large auditorium to see a fattish, balding American with a graying beard, who was the center of attention. He was sitting in a cross-legged position in the midst of flowers, talking in a combination of Eastern, "hip," and psychological language. This was Baba Ram Dass.

Ram Dass was born into an affluent Boston family as Richard Alpert. Educated at Stanford, he taught at Stanford and the University of California at Berkeley. Later he taught psychology and practiced psychotherapy at Harvard. In 1961 he joined his Harvard colleague Timothy Leary in research on mind-altering drugs, notably LSD.

By 1963, Alpert and Leary were dismissed from Harvard. For four years, Alpert continued personal experiments in drugs and publicly defended their use.[75]

In 1967 a visit to India led Alpert from drugs to sympathy with Hindu consciousness techniques. Six months of cold baths at 4 A.M. and study with a guru brought him the title of Baba Ram Dass. Since 1968 he has been in and out of the United States, providing a Hindu religious smorgasbord in lecture series before packed houses. He moves about on college campuses as a sort of Johnny Appleseed of the New Consciousness story.[76] His spiritual autobiography, *Be Here Now*, has sold over one-quarter million copies. Talks given at the Menninger Clinic have been published in a book entitled *The Only Dance There Is*. Another recent book is entitled *Grist for the Mill*. Ram Dass is guru-in-residence at the Lama Foundation near Taos, New Mexico.

A part of Ram Dass' success is his ability to combine his knowledge of Western psychology with his Eastern experiences. He is not a Hindu speaking but a colloquial American charmer who still uses the language of psychology in explaining Hindu concepts. His vernacular speech pattern is well understood by American young people.[77]

BUBBA FREE JOHN (FRANKLIN JONES)

One of the first Westerners to claim Hindu enlightenment was Franklin Jones. In college, Jones tried LSD. Later he studied at a Lutheran seminary. He claimed that he found final enlightenment at a meeting of the Hollywood Vedanta Society. Jones states: "I am Reality. I am God, Brahman, Atman, the One Mind, the Self." [78] His name was changed from Franklin Jones to Bubba Free John after his enlightenment.

Bubba Free John is mentioned in this context because his pilgrimage is similar to that of many middle-class American young people. He teaches in American vernacular style. His book, *Garbage and the Goddess,* reflects his attempt to help young people have intense Hindu spiritual experiences. He is a rather dramatic example of an American seeking to embody Hindu Vedanta religion and New Consciousness techniques.[79]

8
A Concluding Word on Hindu New Consciousness Groups

The movements and figures we have discussed are only a few of the many Hindu New Consciousness groups active in the United States. Each group or person emphasizes a certain spiritual path. Despite its practical physical squalor, India continues to attract those seeking the New Consciousness turn-on. It is a land of religious extremes. It combines color, festivity, and devotional fervor with asceticism and isolated meditation.

As we have seen, Hindu philosophy and religious presupposition are quite different from that of the biblical tradition. For most of the Hindu groups, god in his essence is impersonal. Man, essentially divine, emanates from god; he is not created and essentially personal. Salvation is related to enlightenment and union with god. Sin is ignorance and lack of enlightenment—not rebellion. Immortality is natural or innate. History is cyclical. Matter is essentially illusory.

PART TWO
Buddhist-related New Consciousness Groups
1
Buddhist Groups Challenge America and the World

Fascination with Buddhist-related New Consciousness groups began for me in the 1950s in Cambridge, Massachusetts. Wide publicity was given to an appearance at Massachusetts Institute of Technology by Ruth Fuller Sasaki. She was advertised as the first American in history to become head priestess of a Japanese Zen Temple. Her speech and the following dialogue provided an exciting evening. Coming from a wealthy Chicago home, Ruth Fuller went to Japan to study Zen. Later in New York she married Sasaki, who founded the first Zen institute in America. Mrs. Sasaki later returned to Japan, where she became a Zen priestess. The language and concepts of her speech were difficult to understand but intriguing. I could see how Zen would appeal to American intellectuals.

In the 1960s I went to study in India at Banaras. While there I visited Sarnath where the founder of Buddhism, Gautama, preached his first sermon after he was enlightened or turned on. Later I followed the trail of Buddhism through Thailand, Taiwan, Korea, and finally to Japan.

In Japan everything speaks of Zen—flower arranging, tea ceremonies, gardens, and archery. But there is infinitely more to Buddhism than Zen. In Japan I attempted to understand the most remarkable religious phenomenon of the twentieth century, the growth of Soka Gakkai. Soka Gakkai is a practical form of Buddhism especially attractive to laymen. It advocates chanting for happiness. In its American version it is known as Nicheren Shoshu. More than one quarter of a million Americans are involved in its programs. The center of Soka Gakkai or Nicheren Shoshu is an unforgettable temple on the slopes of Mount Fuji in Japan.

While teaching in California in the late 1960s, I discovered an even more exotic version of the Buddhist New Consciousness groups. As a follow-up to the psychedelic explosion of the sixties, Tibetan or Esoteric or Tantric Buddhism became popular. Already we have looked at its sister group, Tantric Hinduism. *The Tibetan Book of the Dead* is a dramatic expression of some of its ideas. Tantric Buddhism is an affirmation of images, sexuality, and emotionality. From Zen, Nicheren Shoshu, and Tantric Buddhism, evangelical Christians have much to learn as well as much to decry.

2
The Roots of the Buddhist New Consciousness Groups in Historic Buddhism

Already we have looked at representative religious New Consciousness groups stemming from India. Buddhism is best understood as a reform movement with roots in Hinduism. Some call Buddhism an export version of Hinduism.

THE LIFE OF BUDDHA

All of the Buddhist New Consciousness groups relate in some way to a man named Siddhartha Gautama. Born in the sixth century B.C. (around 560) in northern India, he was the son of the ruler of a small Hindu state. Gautama's early life was one of pleasure and luxury. He was protected from evil and suffering. Secretly he slipped out to observe the real world. He was deeply concerned with the poverty and illness that he saw. Soon he left his wife and son to seek the answer to the meaning of life and suffering in an evil world.

Traditional Hindu methods did not seem to have helped Gautama in his quest. Sitting under a huge fig or "bo" tree, at age thirty-five after extended meditation, he achieved enlightenment. The insights received were that all of life is suffering, suffering is caused by desire, and there can be an end to desire. The way or path to extinguished desire is Gautama's path. From the time of his enlightenment, Gautama was known as Buddha, the "Enlightened One" or the "One who is awake." [1]

BASIC BUDDHIST EMPHASES

In Hindu thought, we saw that the soul or self is identical with god or Brahman. Buddha went one step further. If the self is simply the same as the one universal, impersonal Brahman, it is also "no self" (anatman) in any individualistic sense. Man is not a personal being but a bundle of sensations, thoughts, and feelings in a state of flux.

The idea of "no self" is a fundamental clue to the meaning of the four noble truths which Buddha taught. First, according to Buddha, all life is to be seen as suffering. This truth tells us that life is frustrating and unsatisfactory and getting worse and worse. [2]

Second, we are to understand that life is suffering because we try to

50

cling to things such as objects, ideas, and persons which are partial and not permanent. We are constantly anxious over the prospect of losing these objects. We have selfish cravings or desires.

The false idea behind our suffering and grasping is that one is a separate, individual self. Instead of a self or a soul stuck in a body, we are simply five entities (skandhas) temporarily brought together. We are just a mental compilation of five transient conditions: the physical body, one's feelings, ideas or understanding, will, and pure consciousness.[3]

We will come apart because the law of karma, a universal force or law of action and reaction, keeps everything moving and changing. There is nothing like a soul taken from your body when you die and put in another body. The karmic waves, however, which you have made in this life by your actions and thoughts, continue to operate until they put together another set of five elements. If you have left good waves, the new set of elements will be a positive reincarnation. For bad waves, there will be something deplorable reassembled.[4]

Buddha's third truth is that the cessation of suffering and negative reincarnations can be reached by the forsaking of desire.

The fourth truth of Buddha is constituted by his eightfold path. The path involves eight basic steps to stifle desire. This path will help you to end all desire and achieve Nirvana, which means freedom or emancipation. Nirvana is achieved by meditating and acting in harmony with the onrushing waves of the spirit of Buddha. Proper acts which lead to Nirvana include unlimited friendliness, compassion, joy, and even-mindedness. Nirvana means the blowing out of all the fires of desire and the illusions of self which constrict us. One can thus break out into a Nirvanic ocean and ride the tides of the infinite. One can see all and know all. One Buddhist leader states that people are relieved when they learn that they are nothing, that they don't exist.[5]

BUDDHIST DEVELOPMENT

India never really accepted Buddhism. As the Buddhist teaching moved out into the Far Eastern world, it divided into two great traditions.

Southern or Theravada Buddhism remained conservative. It was devoted to the historical Gautama and his atheism and reliance upon self-salvation. It is the Buddhism of Sri Lanka (formerly Ceylon), Burma, Thailand, Cambodia, and Laos.

Northern or Mahayana Buddhism developed in Tibet, China, Korea, and Japan. It is more flexible. The historical Gautama Buddha, although respected, is relatively deemphasized in this type of Buddhism. All reality is full of Buddhas. There are many ways of turning on or finding enlightenment. We will look at three of these ways in our study.

For Northern Buddhism, there are thousands of Buddhas called bodhisattvas or "enlightenment beings." These beings are on their way to final enlightenment. But they delay to help others until all are enlightened. They are skilled and compassionate. A bodhisattva can come down in an apparition or ghost-like body to help the unenlightened in the form of a monk, abbot, orphan, beggar, prostitute, or rich man. He cannot change karma or the law of judgment at a single stroke. But the enlightened being can help you to make new resolutions and eliminate desire by his wise teaching and helpful experiences.[6]

An even more subtle development in Buddhism was the rise of mind-only or consciousness-only Buddhism. According to this view, fundamentally there is only one field of consciousness, which is the Buddha-nature or Nirvana. This consciousness is the basis of each person's existence. We are all Buddhas. We see the world differently, however, because each person carries over karmic impressions from past lives.

The mind-only approach developed various positive means of realizing Nirvana and transforming consciousness. One method, developed by Zen, utilizes still meditation. Another method was developed in Tibet as Tantric Buddhism. It uses sacred and powerful words, gestures, and hard meditation. One of its guide books is the *Tibetan Book of the Dead.*[7]

In the thirteenth century, a zealous leader named Nichiren taught that all forms of Buddha-expression are unified in one writing of Buddha, the *Lotus Sutra.* In chanting the essence of this sutra or teaching, a person can find practical and spiritual help here and now in a simple and almost immediate way.[8]

3
Zen Buddhism

Buddhism came to Japan from China by way of Korea in the early sixth century, A.D. Even today you can see the remnants of the first great Buddhist era at Nara, Japan. In 781, the center of Buddhism was moved to the new city of Heian (modern Kyoto). Here Buddhism became priestly and aristocratic. New warlords rose to power in Japan and moved the capital to Kamakura. This move and the new cultural situation called for different and streamlined versions of Buddhism. Several such versions arose, including Pure Land now popular in Hawaii, Zen with its simple meditation, and Nichiren with its simplified emphasis.[9]

Zen Buddhism appealed to the new warlords because of its unpretentiousness, its lack of elaborate ritual, and its verbal simplicity. The virtues of Zen, such as perfect self-control and indifference to fear or death, also appealed to the warlords.

BASIC CONCEPTS OF ZEN

First of all, Zen should be seen as a spiritual method. The basic idea of Zen is to discover one's true nature beneath the level of impulse and self-consciousness which clouds up our ordinary lives. Zen life and meditation are designed to stop the swirling surface life or activity of one's "monkey mind."

One ancient Zen master, Eisai, developed the Rinzai method of meditation. He used koans or Zen puzzles such as, What is the sound of one hand clapping? These riddles are designed to neutralize the mind, preparing the way for satori or enlightenment.

Another classic master, Dogen, distrusted puzzles. Those following his methods meditate facing a bare wall. They focus on posture and breathing to still the monkey mind.[10]

Zen cuts out, with tremendous discipline, all impulses and all that is not truly natural. The excess must be pruned away to make way for satori, or sudden spontaneous enlightenment. Illusions and ignorance are to die.

This satori experience is unfettered contact with the universal mind. Satori is the mystic state in which you appreciate your own original inseparability with the universe.

In American Zen sessions, after periods of meditation, group chanting is emphasized. The Heart Sutra is often used: "Form is emptiness, and emptiness is form . . . . The wisdom that has gone beyond, and beyond the beyond; O what an awakening, all hail!" [11]

ZEN INFLUENCE ON THE ARTS

For a number of years I have been taking study groups to Japan. For many women a primary motivation for such trips is the opportunity to further their interest in flower arranging, tea ceremonies, and gardens. Few of these Americans realize that the famous Zen cultural contributions are primarily an attempt to promote Zen satori or enlightenment.

Zen monks, in one medium after another, strive to create beauty by pruning away. They seek to allow a single simple core of exquisite naturalness and beauty to stand alone, free of entanglements. Meditation on such an artistic creation should lead toward enlightenment.

Zen-related poetry, haiku, seeks to portray a perfect but understated image in a minimum of words. Haiku is concerned with emotions or an intuitive perception. It uses suggestion and avoids an open statement. A well known haiku poem is by Basho:

An ancient pond,
A frog jumps in—
The sound of water.[12]

Zen painting is mostly white spaces. A bird on a bamboo is represented by a half-dozen strokes of the brush. Details are only suggested, for empty space is inviting. Creative emptiness and suggestive absence are used by Zen artists.

Zen gardens are natural in an irregular sort of way. The raked gravel and moss and gnarled trees are not spaced in formal geometric ways. All is done to reveal the truly natural by pruning and control.

The Zen tea ceremony suggests the absolute in the ordinary. The ceremony has a simplicity which flows from perfect control. The gestures are graceful and seem to be a part of the order of the universe and so of the Buddha nature.[13]

A Zen swordsman is supposed to cause the opponent to flee without striking a blow, simply by the poise of his pose and appearance.

The 1950s were the years of the great explosion of Zen in the United States. Suzuki was its foremost exponent. As a professor at Columbia University in New York City, he exerted great influence among intellectuals. Western converts such as Alan Watts popularized Zen in college circles. I shall never forget a series on Zen led by Alan Watts in which I participated. The sessions took place in the dramatic setting of a houseboat moored in the shadow of the Golden Gate Bridge in the San Francisco area.

An American businessman, Philip Kapleau, became a Zen priest in 1965. His book *The Three Pillars of Zen* is still quite popular in the United States. Kapleau has been a significant force in bringing Zen to the American public.

Zen continues in its appeal to many Westerners. Ten or twelve serious Zen centers with trained masters still provide leadership and training for a quietly growing Zen movement in the United States.[14]

ZEN AND EVANGELICAL CHRISTIANITY

It is obvious that most Zen teachings are quite different from the emphasis of evangelical Christianity. Zen is a self-help religion. For Zen there is no god in the Christian sense. There is no sin, because man himself is a part of the ultimate. There is no need of a divine savior. Man needs only a way-shower. Salvation comes from self-understanding.[15]

Buddhist compassion is that of an enlightened person feeling sorry for the ignorant. For Christianity, man's problem is related to rebellion against God and egocentricity and pride. Salvation for the Christian must come from someone not caught up in man's vicious circle.

4
Nichiren Shoshu (Soka Gakkai)

Perhaps the most religious happening in the twentieth century is the growth of a Buddhist New Consciousness group called Soka Gakkai in Japan and Nichiren Shoshu in America. From a few thousand in 1945 it has grown to twenty million claimed adherents worldwide.[16]

Soka Gakkai is one of 171 newly arisen Japanese religious groups which have developed since 1945. One in three Japanese people has some relationship to one of these groups. Obviously, because of its growth and acceptance, the group which has become most attractive to Occidental Americans is Nichiren Shoshu. It is modern in its appeal, highly organized, and positive in its approach to health and prosperity. It is enthusiastic and simple in its techniques which claim to give Americans power and help.[17]

THE ORIGIN OF NICHEREN SHOSHU

While lecturing and studying at Fukuoka, Japan, I was taken to see a giant statue in a prominent park in the city. Although it was bitterly cold, dozens of people stood around the statue, chanting and kissing the figures depicted on its side. It was a statue of Nichiren Daishonen, a thirteenth-century Buddhist leader.

Nichiren lived in a time of change and disorder in Japan. Buddhism seemed to be lapsing in its power and influence. Furthermore, ordinary people did not understand the complexities of the intricate Buddhist system being taught at that time. The Mongols were threatening Japan. People wanted a simple key to religion and hope for the difficult times. Nichiren proclaimed that he had found the simple and sure key to salvation in the *Lotus Sutra*. One sentence in the *Lotus Sutra* said, "Honestly discard the *provisional* teachings." This seemed to be a call for Nichiren to simplify ponderous Buddhist doctrines.

One of the greatest Buddhist texts is this document called the *Lotus Sutra*. It was said to have been written by Buddha. (Many modern scholars say it was written much later.) It is much like the New Testament book of Revelation in its images. It states that the historical Gautama is but a manifestation of the eternal Buddha-nature.

The mysteries of the *Lotus Sutra* are beyond intellectual comprehension, said Nichiren. Therefore, simple devotion to the *Lotus Sutra* is more important for liberation than meditation or philosophy. It is not necessary that one study the *Lotus Sutra*. The answer for mankind's needs is to chant the Daimoku. The Daimoku is translated as "Glory to the marvelous teaching of the Lotus Sutra." It is claimed that the chanting of this sacred text will put one in harmony with all of the Buddhas mentioned in the *Lotus Sutra*. The chanting will unite mind and body and bring power and bliss. It will produce new material results.

It is important to chant the Daimoku in front of the *Gohonzon*. The *Gohonzon* is a scroll containing the names of the Buddhas in the *Lotus Sutra*. This visual object complements the chant. Focusing on this object as one chants will help to give one the power of the principal Buddhas in the book. Chanting in front of the scroll will turn on the Buddha-nature within you.[18]

Nicheren was fanatic in his devotion to and teaching about the *Lotus Sutra*. If Japan did not reject all other forms of Buddhism and other religions for the *Lotus*, it would suffer calamity. On the other hand, if Japan would follow the *Lotus*, it would become the center of a new world civilization. Nichiren saw his day as a turning point in history.

As his new movement developed, Nichiren taught and his followers believed that he was the Buddha for the new age. Nichiren and the chant constituted a funnel to release into the world a single, clean light. There is only one sutra, one practice, one time, one man (himself), and one country (Japan) to save the world, said Nichiren.[19]

MODERN-DAY REVIVAL OF NICHIREN SHOSHU

The Nichiren movement continued in influence but was relatively quiet from the thirteenth century until 1928. In 1928, a Japanese schoolteacher, Makiguchi, and a young follower, Josei Toda were converted to Nichiren. This was a crucial development. Two years later, these two men founded Soka Gakkai (Value Creation Society). This new organization was based on the teaching of Nichiren. It emphasized that chanting the *Lotus Sutra* would unite all realms of Buddha-nature in the present as a source of power for a joyful, prosperous life here and now.[20]

During World War II, Makiguchi and Toda were imprisoned for their refusal to become involved in nationalist Shinto worship. Makiguchi died in prison but Toda was released. Soon Toda reorganized Soka Gakkai as a lay movement. In the 1950s it became the world's fastest growing religion. In six years it grew from a tiny group to 750,000 households. In the

1970s it claims more than 7.5 million families.[21]

In the 1950s Soka Gakkai (Nichiren Shoshu) practiced "shakubuku." Literally translated, "shakubuku" means to break old Buddhist beliefs and instill the cause of happiness. Shakubuku became notorious as a militant form of recruitment for Nichiren Shoshu. The Nichiren Shoshu movement was intolerant of all other faiths and used many forms of pressure to win and hold converts. Members would chant around the clock at the homes of prospective members until they would break down and join.

Vast rallies were held to promote Nichiren Shoshu. The movement formed a political party, Komeito, which has become the third largest force in Japanese politics. The new head temple of Nichiren Shoshu on the slopes of Mount Fuji is a building of extraordinary architecture, which has received worldwide publicity.

GENERAL TEACHINGS OF NICHIREN SHOSHU

Beyond the specific teachings already mentioned, there are the two general Nichiren Shoshu emphases on happiness and world peace which are important.

The central emphasis of Nichiren Shoshu is on happiness. All three Buddha bodies or forms of expression—absolute essence, the mental world, and the material world—are seen as one. A cause implanted in one of these worlds affects the others. For example, spiritual impulses produce material goods. On the other hand, material goods bring mental happiness. What makes the body happy must do the same for the spirit. The material benefits which derive from chanting are said by Nichiren Shoshu followers to be a practical proof that this unique spiritual-mental-material religion really works.[22]

The members are also taught that world peace will come if enough people chant. Chanting people have no sense of need based on self-deficiency. What goes out from chanting people is only a need to love, relate, and create.

The new civilization which is coming is proclaimed and anticipated in Nichiren Shoshu's cultural activities such as music, drama, and conventions. According to a pronouncement by their leaders, Nichiren Shoshu will lead mankind to achieve permanent peace by the year 2200.[23]

NICHIREN SHOSHU IN AMERICA

The first Occidentals brought into Nichiren Shoshu were the GI's influenced by Japanese girlfriends or wives after World War II. In 1960, President Ikida of Nichiren Shoshu came to America to help spread the new religion. The American head, Sadanaga, changed his name to George

Williams. This is a symbol of Nichiren's amazing adaptability. By 1963 a headquarters was established in the Los Angeles area. The first national convention in Chicago had only fifteen hundred in attendance. By 1966 the growth rate was extremely high. In 1967, the first American Nichiren Shoshu temple was established in California. Growth of Nichiren Shoshu in Hawaii was quite remarkable. More than three hundred thousand are now claimed as United States members of Nichiren Shoshu, most of whom are non-Asiatics.[24]

Almost every major American city has its own NSA *Kaikan,* a combination community center, recruitment headquarters, and place of worship. As the Nichiren Shoshu movement has become more mature, there has been some modification of earlier harsh conversion tactics. Shakubuku is now called solicitation. American work is headed by a general director. The United States headquarters for Nichiren Shoshu is in Santa Monica, California. The basic unit of operation is the district, which meets several times a week. Under the district are groups of some ten members each, which are watched over by experienced individuals. Above the district unit are regional and general chapters. In addition to this hierarchical setup, there are the usual groups such as men and women's divisions, the student bureau, the bureau for pilgrimages to Japan, and the bureau of publications. American temples are located in Washington, D.C., Etiwanda, California, and Hawaii. Occidentals now occupy all places of leadership in Nichiren Shoshu of America. English is the language used in the services.[25]

NICHIREN SHOSHU SERVICES AND CONVENTIONS

Weekly chapter meetings are held either in a Kaikan center or in a home. A typical Nichiren Shoshu chapter meeting is held in a home. Most of the people in attendance are Caucasians, and not Japanese. Upon entering the home for a service, one sees the group gathered facing a dark cabinet-like box, the "butsodon." In this cabinet is a scroll containing the names of the Buddhas described in the *Lotus Sutra.* This scroll is the visual focus of the Nichiren Shoshu religion and is called the *Gohonzon.* Upon conversion, a *Gohonzon* is lent for a lifetime to the convert for a donation. It is installed by district officers in a home ceremony.[26]

Some forty to fifty are present for the typical meeting. The first order on the agenda is the chant of the Daimoku (Glory to the marvelous teaching of the *Lotus Sutra*), or in Japanese, *(Nam Myoho Renge Kyo).* This is the *Lotus Sutra* title. The chanting continues for about forty-five minutes accompanied by drums and the noise of the movement of the Buddhist rosary of 108 beads.

The leader rings a bell to stop the chanting. The next part of the service involves reading in unison certain chapters of the *Lotus Sutra*. It is read in unison in the Sanskrit original with great emotion.

In a rather radical change of style, the next item in the meeting is the informal singing of American hymns and folksongs which are sung in an informal way. The words of the songs have been changed. The primary emphasis is on the virtue of chanting and promulgating Nichiren Shoshu. "I've been doing shakabuku" (aggressive evangelism) is sung to the tune of "I've Been Working on the Railroad." One chant is like a pep yell, "Let's go NSA, NSA all the way."

Visitors are introduced. For their benefit, a brief account of Nichiren Shoshu as the true Buddhism is given. The leader points out that Nichiren Shoshu goes back in its origins three thousand years to Buddha. It was developed as a specific religion, however, by Nichiren in the thirteenth century A.D. Only since 1945 has it been available to make all of the people of the world happy. Nichiren Shoshu alone can bring world peace, for world peace must begin within. Nichiren Shoshu is a simple faith and for everybody, smart or dumb.

Usually a period of promotion is given describing the advantages of a pilgrimage to Japan to visit the world headquarters of Nichiren Shoshu at the foot of Mount Fuji. At this sacred center, the original *Gohonzon* made by Nichiren, as well as Nichiren's tooth, can be seen. This *Gohonzon* is the supreme object of worship for Nichiren Shoshu.

Perhaps the most impressive part of the meeting is the giving of testimonials. The people present can hardly be restrained from speaking at the same time. Most of the testimonies have to do with benefits that come from the simple practice of chanting the Daimoku. One girl reports that she chanted and got a new house and one hundred dollars. A young man tells of a new job and getting his guitar fixed free. Others tell of deliverance from drugs, alcoholism, and marital problems. All speakers tell of the material good luck and happiness that come from chanting. All of the testimonies tell of personal change and the acquisition of power. In fact one housewife candidly acknowledges that she was not seeking spiritual enlightenment when she took up chanting. "I wanted money to buy food. I wanted my husband to find work and my son to be healthy." All three wishes, she says, were promptly granted.[27] Visitors are urged to try chanting on a test basis since it is scientific, based on cause and effect. Try it for one hundred days, the leaders plead.

Announcements are made about classes to help people chant the hard words of the *Lotus Sutra*. The last emphasis of the meeting is on outreach. Instructions are given for solicitation or witnessing and for selling the

Nichiren Shoshu paper. The entire service is characterized by happy smiles, friendliness, dynamic energy, chanting, and music.

For active members, strict adherence to chanting schedules is required. Most members must attend daily meetings and actively recruit new members.

The annual conventions draw thousands of participants who fill the largest available convention centers. At the conventions the dynamics of the Nichiren Shoshu movement come out in a dramatic way. These large meetings are filled with fun and festivity. Great parades are held with bands and floats. Programs combine chanting, addresses, and musical performances. Charter flights bring delegates from most major metropolitan areas. Delegates wear identical clothes. Cheering is combined with worship. The people are affirmative. Central to all other activity is the chanting. The chanting of the Daimoku unites the movement to its roots in Buddhism and Nichiren. The members are reminded that their faith alone will save the world, bring peace, and provide the basis for mankind's "Third Civilization."[28]

AN EVALUATION OF NICHIREN SHOSHU OF AMERICA

From the perspective of biblical religion, Nichiren Shoshu falls far short. Christianity never equates the will of God for human life with immediate material satisfaction. In Nichiren Shoshu one does not find a transcendent and holy god who calls for repentance and change to conform to a prophetic way of life, such as that incarnated in Jesus Christ.

Nichiren Shoshu is close to magic in some of its emphases. Whatever you want, whether morally constructive or not, is granted if you chant. One woman, evidently a prostitute, said in a recent Nichiren Shoshu meeting that she had picked up more clients because she chanted. This sort of emphasis reveals that Nichiren Shoshu is a manipulationist type of religion.

Evangelical Christianity would also question the discounting of study and evaluation in favor of mere chanting. Jesus said that we are to love God with mind, soul, and body. A wrong kind of intolerance as contrasted with a right kind of zeal is inherent in the Nichiren Shoshu movement. Techniques of recruitment used have long been deplored by sensitive Christians.

Lessons can be learned from Nichiren Shoshu successes. Framed in a more authentic world view and tempered by moderation, many Nichiren Shoshu emphases can be adopted for constructive use.

Qualities and emphases worth adopting include simplicity of techniques, concreteness of method, unity of mind and matter, power of the arts, and enthusiasm. People need to belong and Nichiren has shown the attraction of a strong sense of fellowship. The power of positive thinking is an obvious emphasis that has much truth.

Religion is universal. Religion is powerful. Nichiren Shoshu reveals to us that religion can easily be prostituted for less than authentic ends.

5
Esoteric (Tantric) and Tibetan Buddhism in America

In our discussion of Tantric Hinduism, enough material was given to provide an understanding of the attraction and emphases of the Tantric tradition. Buddhist as well as Hindu religious leaders have brought the Tantric emphases to America. Originally nurtured in the Himalayas, mountains are the center of the Tantric sacred geography. This tradition of esoteric Buddhism was brought to Japan in the ninth century A. D. From Japan as well as Tibet it has been exported to the United States.

There are a number of American versions of Tantric Buddhism. Elaborate rituals and sexuality are used as a means to enlightenment. Deities are visualized. Such a Buddhism has some parallels with neopaganism and ceremonial magic.[29]

Chogyam Trungpa Tulku was once the supreme abbot of one of Tibet's strongest Buddhist sects. He was called the incarnate lama. Driven out of Tibet by the Communists, Chogyam has established Naropa Institute in Boulder, Colorado. His ambition is to expand Naropa into the Buddhist University of America. Many versions of Buddhism are taught at Naropa. Chogyam's Tantric teachings are described as both an intellectual and a practical psychology based on meditation.[30]

PART THREE
Islamic-related New Consciousness Groups

In a course on world religions, I was told that Islam was the one great nonmystical religion. God or Allah was One and was to be submitted to—not mystically experienced.

On a trip to the famous Christian monastery at the foot of Mount Sinai, I heard about a different side of Muhammad, the founder of Islam. Official Islam tends to picture Muhammad as rather legalistic and dogmatic. Muhammad himself, however, had a mystical side. He had great respect for the Christian mystics in their hidden monasteries. It is said that he sent word to his forces to protect the safety of the Christian monks at the monastery at Mount Sinai.

My knowledge of the mystical side of Islam was further enlarged by the visit to my class on mysticism of a brilliant English professor who is also a Sufi leader. In her lecture she detailed the remarkable influence of the mystical group called Sufism. This group, she pointed out, has its roots in Islam. She further indicated that many of the recent New Consciousness groups such as Subud, the Lovers of Meher Baba, Arica, and the Gurdjieff-Ouspensky group (G-O) are greatly influenced by Sufism. No account of New Consciousness groups would be complete without a brief discussion of these Islamic-related developments.

1
The Islamic Background of Sufism and Related New Consciousness Groups

Like Judaism and Christianity, Islam is a religion originating in the Near East and among Semitic people. Moreover, like these religions of the Bible, it is strongly monotheistic and emphasizes a unique revelation from the one God. It shares much of Old Testament history and claims Abraham as its great patriarch. Moreover, it betrays some influences from Christianity. Although the youngest of the world's great religions, it is one of the largest. Approximately one-half billion people follow Islam.[1]

Islam means "submission," so Islam is a religion of submission to the will of God. *Muslim* means "a submitter" or "one who submits" to God.

Non-Muslims usually consider the prophet Muhammad as the founder of Islam. Muslims, however, prefer to call Muhammad God's messenger and the interpreter and exemplar of the Koran, the holy book, which is eternal.

Muhammad was born in Mecca, Arabia, in A.D. 570. As a youth, he was an attendant on caravans. On these journeys he probably had some limited contact with Christians and Jews. At the age of twenty-five, Muhammad married his rich employer, a widow. When forty years of age, Muhammad began to experience visions by which he received his prophetic call.

Instructed by the angel Gabriel, as he claimed, to proclaim God's message, Muhammad began to preach a strong monotheism, or belief in one God. He also denounced the idolatrous polytheism (worship of many gods) and primitive religion of Arabia.

The visions and revelations of Muhammad were recorded as the Koran, which, along with the unwritten prophecies or sunna, became the basis for a new religion, militant and bent on conquering the world for God (Allah).

Unlike the Hebrew-Christian Bible, the Koran is not a collection of diverse material from over a thousand years or so. It was all received or delivered in a period of no more than twenty-two years. According to Islamic teaching, the Koran came through one man in private sessions with God and his angel, Gabriel. The Koran is not a life of Muhammad or a book of history. It is primarily a book of the proclamation of the oneness and sovereignty of God and of man's need to submit to him. The sunna tell how the Koran is to be applied to life in an objective way.[2]

Belief in Allah is the fundamental faith of the orthodox Muslim. This belief is a zealous unitarianism proclaiming that God is undivided, having no partner or associate to share his being. Muslims consider Christians polytheists.

In Muslim belief, God is absolutely different from man. His revelation is actually a disclosure of his will rather than his nature. In his essential being, Allah remains unknown.

Belief in angels is also essential to the Muslim faith. If God is absolutely different from man, then some being between God and man is necessary to bear God's message to man.

Belief in prophets or apostles is another fundamental article of Muslim faith. There are many prophets or apostles, including Noah, Abraham, Ishmael, Moses, Elijah, and Jesus, and all of these must be allowed. But Muhammad is the greatest of all. He is not deified. Muhammad is the last, or seal, of the prophets. He supersedes all previous prophets. Islam thus claims to be the ultimate or super-religion because it is the simplest and clearest—the restoration of original monotheism.[3]

SUNNITES AND ORTHODOXY

As already indicated, my primary knowledge of Islam has been through the eyes of the more orthodox or Sunna tradition. The largest group in Islam, the Sunnites, have as their fundamental authority the Muslim law. This law is interpreted by consensus of learned men who base their decisions on tradition and analogy. This tradition is rather legalistic and stresses putting all of life under God and the Koran.[4]

SHIITES AND THE COMING IMAM

The Sha division of Islam is smaller but has many followers. It is the official Islam of Iran, much of Iraq, and has a strong representation in such countries as Pakistan, India, Yemen, and Lebanon.

The Shiites do not accept the first three caliphs as true leaders of Islam. For them, the first divinely appointed and authoritative leader (Imam) or teacher was Ali. Ali was Muhammad's cousin and son-in-law, having married his daughter, Fatima. After Ali came twelve other Imams. All were mysteriously killed except the last. The twelfth is the Mahdi, or Imam for all time. This twelfth Imam is said to still be living in an invisible state. In the fullness of time he will reappear to bring justice to the earth. This Shiite idea has carried over directly to the Baha'i religion. The Baha'is claim that their leader is the promised Imam.[5]

2
Sufism

MYSTICISM WITHIN ISLAM

In addition to orthodox or dominant Islam there is a mystical or New Consciousness Islamic emphasis. In the West this tradition is known as Sufism. Its followers are called Sufis. Their God is the same God as the one described in the Koran and tradition. As we shall see, there are two emphases within Sufism. One group says that they are only seeking to cultivate immediate communion with Allah. Another group moves closer to pantheistic forms of mystical absorption. This group almost passes over the line fixed between the Creator and his creation.[6]

THE ORIGINS AND RISE OF SUFISM

Sufi scholars see at least three reasons for the rise of the mystical emphasis in Islam. The first factor is the Sufi understanding of the inner life of Muhammad himself. They see Muhammad as a man who knew God intimately, even to moments of trance and rapture in fellowship with God.

Muhammad as a mystic. In the Koran, there are references to Muhammad wrapping himself in a mantle. The Sufis see this engirdling cloak or mantle as a means to, and a symbol of, Muhammad's inner mystical experience and union with God. By means of the mantle, Muhammad deliberately concentrated his mind and freed it from sense distractions. Muhammad's life was marked by severe discipline and special prayers after midnight.[7]

Other references in the Koran are seen as indications of a night journey of Muhammad to Jerusalem and an ascension to heaven. In heaven God showed him sights not seen by ordinary mortals.[8]

Orthodox Islamic tradition emphasizes the moral laws which Muhammad decreed. For the Sufis, Muhammad from the beginning was a passionate lover of God, seeking mystical union with him. The Sufis aspire to imitate Muhammad's alleged mystical techniques and union with God. This mystical path was Muhammad's perfection of the timeless way known to the mystics of all generations.[9]

Reaction against corruption and luxury. A second factor in the

66

emergence of the Sufis was a reaction to the moral laxities, luxuries, and corruption of the Umayyad Caliphate in the Islamic metropolis at Damascus. In fact, the repudiation of the worldliness of establishment Islam in the eighth century is the probable explanation of the term *Sufi*. *Sufi* is derived from "suf" (wool). Wearing wool was a rebuke, in its simplicity, to the silks and satins of the Damascus court. The Sufis also wore wool as a symbol of their warm and intimate devotion to the desert simplicity and pure devotion of Muhammad himself.[10]

Reaction against abstraction and legalism. A third factor in the rise of Sufism was discontent with the abstraction, dryness, and legalism of Islamic law and dogma as it developed in the tenth and eleventh centuries A.D. Reason as used by the theologians was seen as proud and contentious. Sufi inwardness made of greatest importance the personal relation of faith and love to God. Orthodox Islam obviously failed to satisfy the demands of the Sufi devotional spirit.[11]

REPRESENTATIVE FIGURES IN SUFI HISTORY

An early Sufi, Rabi'ah of Basra (d. A.D. 801) was said to have been on fire with love, ardent desire, and passion for God. She taught a disinterested love of God, without fear of punishment or reward. Junayd of Baghdad (d. A.D. 910) taught "Fana" or a loss of will or self in union with God. The most famous pupil of Junayd was Al-Hallaj. In 922, Al-Hallaj was tortured and executed in Baghdad for saying, "I am the Real" or "the creative Truth." These statements were regarded as blasphemy since truth and reality are attributes of God alone. Al-Hallaj taught the possibility of perfect union with God, claiming to follow the example of Jesus. He pressed beyond the allowable communion and illumination to a claim of complete absorption in God.[12]

Perhaps Omar Khayyam is the best known Persian mystic in English-speaking circles, but Al-Ghazali (d. A.D. 1111) is the greatest Sufi. Born in Iran, Al-Ghazali lived and taught in Baghdad. Revolting against traditional rational theology, he studied Sufi writings. In his own writings, Al-Ghazali kept the Sufi ardor and love, yet gave it a disciplined pattern. He reestablished theology on the basis of personal mystical experience.[13]

THE PRACTICES OF THE SUFIS

Practice or experience is all-important for the Sufis. They say, "Come where I am; I can show you the way" in contrast to the orthodox call: "Believe what I teach; I can tell you the orthodox truth."

By the eleventh century, the idea that one should submit to one's spiritual guide or master gained force among the Sufis. The master concept is an Islamic parallel to the Hindu guru. The guides showed followers the inward meaning of the normative devotional practices of Islam such as fasting, prayers, and almsgiving. The Sufi way taught by the masters consisted of three main grades: the novice, the traveler, and the attainer.

Sufi masters, organized into great Sufi orders, developed special ecstatic techniques for knowing God. The orders originally gathered around some great master and his devotional techniques. One such technique was a repetition of the ninety-nine beautiful names of God, aided by prayer beads. Such repetitions helped concentrate the mind and produce an emotional state of swaying and chanting.[14]

Another well-known technique was the dervish. The dervish involves the use of rhythmic recitation and rhythmic movements of the body to induce concentration on God and divorcement from the physical world. The dervishes whirl with closed eyes, to the music of flutes, drums, and strings, seeking union with the divine. Loud rhythmic praises of Allah are sung. Some Sufis collapse in ecstasy and cry out in various tongues. In Java, some of the Sufis even stab themselves with iron daggers at the height of the ecstasy. Against this background, we will not be surprised when we note the techniques of the modern movement called Subud.[15]

RECENT DEVELOPMENTS IN SUFISM

The Sufi orders still exist. Some Sufi groups have been suppressed in countries like Turkey because of their revolutionary overtones. Other modern Islamic governments see the whole Sufi attitude as superstitious and nonproductive. Sufi orders, however, have had great success in spreading Islam in India and Indonesia. Today Sufi orders are an important factor in spreading Islam in Africa. Ironically, as we shall see, Sufism has been discovered and much appreciated by people outside of Islam.[16]

In the West, Sufism has considered itself as having significance beyond its sectarian Islamic origins. Modern Sufi leaders state that Sufi techniques portray the universal process by which man can attain truth, beauty, and God. The Sufis are thus trying to make their distinctive experience independent and of unconditioned universal validity. This emphasis makes them rather heterodox in orthodox Islamic lands. But this universalistic trend has resulted in the Sufis becoming an important part of the New Consciousness movement in the West.[17]

EVALUATION OF SUFISM

From a theological perspective, the Sufis are always in danger of sinking into a monism. Monism teaches the identity of the divine and the

68

human. One Sufi has written, "Glory to me, how Great is my majesty." The important distinction between God as subject and man as object is prone to disappear in some Sufi circles.[18]

The lack of rational concern easily led into bizarre aberrations and excesses among early Sufis. The Sufi doctrines of passivity and veneration of saints in some cases led to apathy and crude superstition. Yet at its best Sufism has produced many remarkable works of piety. A leading contemporary exponent of Sufism is Idries Shaw. He has translated many of the tales and parables of Sufism into English. Prominent Western scholars, such as the psychologist Robert E. Ornstein, have found the methods of contemporary Sufism of great significance.[19]

In contemporary New Consciousness circles, the interest is in more than a knowledge of the history of Sufism. The primary concern is with the secrets of the Sufi masters. How did they alter consciousness? What were their techniques of consciousness raising? How did they attain super-consciousness? Some of these techniques have been brought to the West by Gurdjieff, Subud, and Oscar Ichaza and the Arica movement.

3
Lovers of Meher Baba

As the Sufis moved east to India they had significant influence. They adopted, however, some Hindu emphases. One example of the Sufi teaching being influenced by Hinduism is seen in the career of Meher Baba.

Born in India in 1894 to Persian parents, Meher Baba attended a Christian high school. While in college a Sufi saint kissed him on the forehead and revealed to him that he was an avatar. As we have seen in our study of the Hindu-related groups, from the Indian perspective, an avatar is a human manifestation of god in the lineage of Jesus, Krishna, Rama, and Buddha.

Meher Baba's writings were heavily influenced by Sufism. His book *God Speaks* celebrates the love of god. Since Baba claimed to be an incarnation of god, being in Baba's presence was to be in god's presence. According to Baba lovers, god revealed himself in all his glory. Union with god is achieved through surrender to Baba.[20]

TEACHINGS OF MEHER BABA

Meher Baba exemplifies an extreme development of Sufi and Hindu philosophies. Baba saw himself as the final incarnation of god in this particular cycle of time. Baba made such statements as "I am the Christ. I am infinite consciousness, I am everything. I am the personification of the universal consciousness. I am immanent in everyone."

The Sufi emphasis on feeling and mystical love is clearly seen in the Baba writings. Baba lovers are urged to suspend all rational thoughts and simply love Meher Baba. If you lose your identity in Baba you will find that you eternally were Baba.[21]

DEVELOPMENTS IN THE BABA MOVEMENT

Baba's techings are popular in the United States. Many college campuses and cities have chapters of Baba lovers meeting regularly. Baba centers are on both coasts and in Florida. The largest Baba center and the main American shrine is in Myrtle Beach, South Carolina. Meher Baba himself spent time in South Carolina on each of his five visits to the United States.

From 1925 until his death in 1969, Meher Baba did not speak. His communication was restricted to an alphabet board and hand gestures. He claimed that before his death he would break his silence by speaking the one word which would spiritualize the world and open a new age of love. This he did not do. Some followers believe that he may yet come again to fulfill his promise.[22]

A San Francisco organization, Sufism Reoriented, claims that Meher Baba is an important avatar. This organization, however, is also concerned with the broader Sufi tradition.

Meher Baba book stores continue as centers of Baba loving. The Myrtle Beach center still entertains many pilgrims. Some claim that Baba still communicates his love to them from his nonphysical state.[23] Whatever its future, the Baba movement is a dramatic and perhaps distorted example of the Sufi celebration of god's love and its emphasis on emotional mysticism.

EVALUATION OF THE BABA MOVEMENT

From a Christian perspective, only Jesus Christ, whose teachings are seen as vindicated by his life, death, and resurrection, could appropriately make such claims as those made by Meher Baba. Furthermore, oneness with Jesus Christ does not diminish personal identity. In fact, for the Christian, a person's individuality is heightened in Christian conversion. Each person as he is loved by God in Jesus Christ has personal individualized worth.[24]

4
Gurdjieff-Ouspensky Groups (G-O)

LIFE OF GURDJIEFF

Some of the techniques and insights of Sufism have been brought to the West by one of the most mysterious persons in the area of New Consciousness studies—George Gurdjieff (1872-1949). Born in Russia, near the Persian border, he traveled throughout the Middle and Far East. He learned many of the techniques which he later taught from the Sufis and Tantric Buddhists. Some of the comic stories found in Gurdjieff's *Beelzebub's Tales to His Grandson* remind us of Sufi tales and parables.[25]

Gurdjieff was known as a sly businessman who accumulated fortunes—oftentimes by questionable means. Driven out of Russia at the time of the Communist revolution, Gurdjieff bought an estate near Paris. In the early 1920s he established on the estate an Institute for the Harmonious Development of Man.

P.D. Ouspensky was a well-known Russian mathematician who became Gurdjieff's closest disciple and interpreter. Ouspensky's *In Search of the Miraculous* is seen as the best systematic presentation of Gurdjieff's thought. Utilizing the names of both Gurdjieff and Ouspensky, the groups studying their teachings are often called the G-O groups. Gurdjieff's chief English follower was J. G. Bennet.[26]

THE TEACHINGS OF GURDJIEFF

The heart of the teaching of Gurdjieff is related to his techniques of awakening a person's dormant consciousness or potentiality. Gurdjieff called his approach the "Fourth Way." This fourth or highest level can be induced by the experiences of music, dance, and physical labor. The "waking up" experience takes supreme effort following careful instruction and guidance. It requires a strict master, deliberate suffering, and a supporting group of fellow students. According to Gurdjieff, not to follow such a disciplined way means devolution, decline, and degeneration.[27]

PRACTICES OF GURDJIEFF-OUSPENSKY GROUPS

As already indicated, awakening and development require strict discipline according to Gurdjieff. Physical labor was one technique for awaken-

72

ing and all people at his Institute, rich and poor, did hard manual labor under Gurdjieff's direction. Regulated food consumption was a part of Gurdjieff's program. The diet prescribed for followers at the Institute was strange and generally sparse. The exception was a weekly banquet held in a grand style.

Severe physical and emotional testings, including therapeutic abuse and irritation, were employed. Imitating the Zen masters, shock was often administered to followers.

In the evenings, Gurdjieff would usually speak to the Institute members. Then would come the "sacred gymnastics." Utilizing techniques gained from the Sufis, the people would engage in ecstatic dancing, often whirling. The intricate group dances required rigorous coordination of limbs and exacting teamwork.[28]

For more advanced students, Gurdjieff taught the use of a kind of Mantra Yoga. Other unusual techniques utilized included standing nude in front of a mirror for fifteen minutes a day.[29]

THE INFLUENCE OF GURDJIEFF

The influence of Gurdjieff continues in the United States. He is now recognized as one of the West's pioneer gurus. Although he saw the life of the average man as nonsensical and meaningless, Gurdjieff taught positive techniques for change. In fact, in his techniques we can now recognize the seeds of many contemporary developments.[30]

In terms of size and number, G-O groups continue to grow. Today there are groups studying Gurdjieff's teachings in most of the major cities of Europe and America. One serious and important center of study is the Gurdjieff Foundation of New York City. The New York center, as well as the other groups, state that they intend to continue the Gurdjieff tradition. They will continue to try to create a mental-emotional-physical experience leading to an awakening from what they call "sleep."[31]

EVALUATION OF GURDJIEFF

Much can be learned from the G-O groups about the importance of physical, mental, and emotional discipline and techniques.

From a Christian perspective, the Gurdjieff movement lacks vertical dimensions. In Calvinist terms, only through God-knowledge can a person gain authentic self-knowledge.

In certain ways, the Gurdjieff system resembles some of the heresies that confronted early Christianity. One example would be the incipient Gnosticism which the apostle Paul discussed and criticized in the letter to the Colossians.[32]

5
Subud

As Sufism moved east from its Arabian homeland, it became more mystical and ecstatic. When it reached lush, tropical Indonesia, it found a different background and milieu. This new cultural climate influenced the development of Sufism. Indonesian Sufi dervishes, for example, are known for their religious ecstasy and strange circular dances. In this Indonesian milieu, the highly emotional New Consciousness group called Subud found its origin. It is not surprising that the Subud "latihan" experience is one of the most emotional of the New Consciousness initiation ceremonies. Some Gurdjieff followers maintain that Subud is the logical end product of the work begun by Gurdjieff.[33]

EARLY HISTORY AND DEVELOPMENT OF SUBUD

The founder of Subud is an Indonesian named Mohammed Subuh (b. 1901). Subuh is now generally called Bapak or Father. As a child and teenager, Bapak consulted many Sufi leaders. None satisfied him with their teachings. Some of the Sufis suggested that he was a unique person destined for great things in the religious realm and already beyond their help. Unsure of his spiritual destiny, Bapak became a civil servant and lived a quiet life.[34]

In 1925, at age twenty-four, Bapak had a rather spectacular initiation experience. A ball of light descended and appeared to enter his head, filling him with light and vibrations. People claimed to have seen the light emanating from his head for a distance of several miles. For three years he experienced this light and felt the vibrations. His life was vibrant and filled with joy and energy.[35]

At age twenty-seven, in 1928, this spontaneous and perpetual experience of light stopped. The following period in Bapak's life was one of darkness, spiritually speaking. In the absence of definite spiritual purpose, he continued as a normal businessman. As best he could, he counselled people in need.

In 1933, at age thirty-two, Bapak came to a new understanding of his mission in a mystical experience. He announced that he was called to share his original spiritual experience with other people through direct contact and witnessing. Through contact with him, direct transmission of energy could be realized. If the person in need would respond to Bapak's contact in simple love and surrender, a unique experience could be found. The receiver's intellectual mind must not be allowed to interfere.[36]

Word of Bapak's powers spread. A Sufi teacher in Java sent people to Bapak to receive this energy. The group who responded and were helped constituted the beginning of the Subud movement. The word *Subud* is derived from the Sanskrit and means living according to the will of god through enlightenment and teaching. For twenty-five years the Subud movement quietly spread throughout the island of Java.[37]

SUBUD COMES WEST

It was J. G. Bennett, active in British New Consciousness circles, who introduced Gurdjieff's teachings to England. Bennett reports that Gurdjieff himself, as he neared death, told him, "After I go another will come. You will not be left alone." On trips to the East, Bennett was told by holy men that he was to become an English John the Baptist and be the forerunner of a new savior or spiritual deliverer who was soon to appear. Bennett was further convinced that there was to be no real headway spiritually in the world until mankind's "higher emotional center" was opened.

The next development came when Bennett heard of the impact Bapak was making in the Far East. Bennett became convinced that Bapak was the new messiah foretold by Gurdjieff.[38]

In 1957 Bapak was invited to England to set up his court at Bennett's big home near London. This home was the Gurdjieff center of England. Soon this Gurdjieff center was swept by enthusiasm for "latihan," the new emotional initiation experience brought by Bapak from Indonesia. Almost overnight the Gurdjieff followers gave up the words, talk, hard discipline, and grueling physical labor required by Gurdjieff for the immediate release promised in latihan.[39]

British newspapers and media spread the news of Bapak and Subud around the world. Spiritual revelations and miracle cures were described as flowing from the impact of the new spiritual leader from the East. The film star Eva Bartok was reported to have been healed of a childbirth complication in a latihan experience led by Bapak himself.[40]

The international Subud movement was underway. A new comet which appeared was declared to be a signal of the importance of the coming of Subud to the West. Bapak immediately embarked on a lengthy world tour. Wherever he went he drew frenzied press attention. In 1959 an

International Subud Congress was held in England.

THE GROWTH OF SUBUD

The growth of Subud is quite spectacular considering that it is a nonhierarchical movement. It has become one of the most widespread of the "new" New Consciousness groups, with centers in over sixty countries. In the United States there are more than seventy Subud centers. Its members come from all age and cultural groups. Its followers claim that Subud is the world's first truly international religion.

EMPHASES OF SUBUD

From our study of Sufism, we have some background for understanding Subud. According to Bapak, there is a superior energy or divine force available to man called god. This higher energy cannot be understood, appropriated, or even clearly desired by unaided man who lives in his lower nature. This divine energy, or god, is available only to the *whole* man. Both the intellect and the feelings must be involved. There is nothing to learn or do. All that is required is complete surrender to the higher energy under the proper guidance.[41]

Subud sees man as a receptacle and transmitter for both animal and divine forces. The latihan or initiation experience is a process of purification. In this experience a person is gradually freed from the dominance of animal energies. To achieve this freedom, a person need only *open* himself to the higher energies called god. Bapak and his helpers are channels of higher energies. Latihan arises spontaneously in an individual from within after contact has been made with a person in whom latihan is already established. The intellect must be subordinate in latihan since the mind is a coarser quality of energy.[42]

In the United States Subud circles, one prepares for latihan by registering as a probationer. Once a week for three months, you go to an appointed building and remain outside the latihan room and listen to the people undergoing latihan inside. At the end of the three-month period, a helper will read words from Bapak's writings to you in a cloakroom. Then you are admitted to the darkened latihan room itself. After removing your watch and glasses, you are told by the helper to close your eyes and begin. The beginner is told not to try to control his body or mind. In most cases people undergoing latihan begin to shout, croon, leap, weep, speak in tongues, or utter wordless chants.[43]

At times the psychic blast of the latihan experience becomes unmanageable. It is an important task of the helper to note when someone's latihan appears to be out of control and help bring it to an immediate conclusion. Bapak insists that latihan is different from a trance or hypnotic state. One is supposed to be fully conscious throughout the experience.[44] Each latihan lasts about half an hour. Three per week is the maximum number of latihans allowed.

It should be noted that latihan is more Eastern than the approach of Gurdjieff. More typical Western qualities such as intellectual precision, scientific analysis, and driving energy are emphasized by Gurdjieff groups.

Subud members claim that participation in latihan opens up the person one really is or the person as he is known to god. Testimonies tell of the falling away of undesirable habits and the gaining of buoyancy and power as a result of latihan. Others report physical and emotional healings.[45]

A Subud technique called *testing* relates to practical problems such as marriage, sex, friendship, and jobs. The question or problem is posed in one's mind and then latihan is commenced. The answer to the problem posed comes in terms of inner feelings, new perceptions, and different patterns of thought.

By and large, testing replaces or supplements any pronounced rules of conduct. If general principles of conduct are given to Subud members, they are to be seen in terms of their instrumentality toward "inner growth." [46]

ORGANIZATION OF SUBUD

The organization of Subud is relatively simple. There are national and regional boards. Each center has a board of directors. The helpers or spiritual guides must be appointed by Bapak or his representatives. In addition to the latihan, business meetings are held. One other regular meeting is known as a "salamatan" or feast. Since there is an anti-intellectual bias in Subud, any discussion with outsiders concerning the meaning of Subud is avoided in public meetings. In latihan nothing occurs that is to be remembered.[47]

THE SIGNIFICANCE OF SUBUD

Subud is an excellent example of a nonrational New Consciousness group. It teaches that with the right key or technique, one can short circuit oneself into a higher kind of consciousness. This experience will make life suddenly meaningful. Subud is similar in some ways to recent psychotherapeutic methods such as Primal Therapy.[48]

Unlike most Hindu and Buddhist New Consciousness groups which we have discussed, Subud does not provide tangible symbols or word formulas in its techniques. One does not so much see or hear, but rather one feels and senses. Subud followers have a difficult time describing the force that enters them in the latihan. Terms such as *love, incredible freedom,* and *great space inside* are used. Some say that the force experienced is heavy and others say that it is light.[49]

CHRISTIAN EVALUATION OF SUBUD

Christianity is unique in its delicate combination of historical roots and personal experience. Ethical fruits are important in judging the results of any reported mystical experience. Christianity teaches that the Holy Spirit has come to make real and carry out the implications of that which Jesus Christ taught and did in his earthly life and ministry. The Spirit gives spiritual gifts, but the gifts are primarily to edify or build up the church and its mission. The more spectacular spiritual gifts, such as speaking in tongues, are to be kept under rational, moral, and emotional control. The primary purpose of Christian experience is to make a person more Christlike. This delicate balance between the ethical, historical, rational, and emotional is not found by the Christian in Subud teachings and practices.

For the Christian faith, God is not the sum total of natural impulses in which view the terms *good* and *evil* have no meaning. God is the Creator, revealed historically through concrete acts in history. Personal experiences with God and his power cannot be divorced from his character and redemptive purposes.

6
Arica (Oscar Ichazo)

A fascinating example of Sufi influence is seen in one of the latest New Consciousness groups, Arica. This group was founded in 1971 by Bolivian guru Oscar Ichazo.

Word came to the United States that Ichazo had developed a super-package that could take people to new levels of consciousness. Some Americans went to Chile where Ichazo was living to investigate. Convinced of its importance by what they found in Chile, forty-two Americans formed a teaching group in New York City. This group sponsored a major and lengthy teaching appearance for Ichazo in New York City. Ichazo's program is called Arica. The name *Arica* means "open door" in Quechua, the language of the Bolivian Indians.

LIFE OF OSCAR ICHAZO

Although Ichazo owes much to the Sufis, he actually synthesizes New Consciousness techniques from many sources. As a young man, Oscar was an epileptic. Unsuccessful in finding help from Christianity, he began a life-long study of New Consciousness techniques. At age nineteen he joined a Gurdjieff group in Buenos Aires, Argentina. This group introduced him to Sufism, Zen, and the Kabbalah. Next Ichazo went to the Far and Middle East to seek out the Sufi, Hindu, and Buddhist leaders. Returning to Chile, he developed his own distinctive consciousness-altering program.[50]

THE TEACHING OF ARICA

Basic to Oscar Ichazo's teaching is the concept of divine unity. According to Ichazo, man has lost unity with god by falling prey to the ego and its traps and its passions. For Ichazo, the current crisis in Western, secular society is rooted in its lack of unity with the divine. The Arica program attempts to show how the ancient Sufi, Buddhist, Taoist, Hindu, and Christian disciplines can be brought up-to-date to help man achieve unity with the Divine.[51]

Ichazo's initial New York Arica course was for three months, six days a week, fourteen hours a day. The cost for the course was three thousand dollars. The course was intended for leaders who would go out to spread the Arica techniques to others. Among techniques taught were adaptations from Hatha Yoga, diet programs, chanting of Sufi music, religious dance, and physical exercises. Mantras were chanted and meditation practices taught which involved staring at colorful wall symbols called yantras. There was also an emphasis on imagination exercises, group work, and karma cleaning (confession and desensitization).[52]

Ichazo sees Arica's primary mission as effecting a reconciliation of mysticism and the modern world. It also seeks to blend Eastern and Western disciplines. The Arica program is designated by some of its proponents as a university for altered states of consciousness. The program is not promoted as one primarily designed for personal self-improvement. Graduates are to become missionary in their concern. According to Ichazo, humanity must alter its consciousness and achieve divine unity or face extinction.[53]

THE GROWTH OF ARICA

Since the initial course for leaders was held in New York City, Arica teachers have spread out over the United States to most major cities. Ads in newspapers and radio commercials open many doors. Summer programs are available in various mountain retreats and resort areas. Arica is one of the latest and most sophisticated New Consciousness groups to find a place in the United States.[54]

7
Baha'i

For a number of years I have been conducting study tours to Israel. Oftentimes we sail into the harbor of Haifa on a cruise ship. The first question asked is, What is the beautiful gold-domed building on the side of Mount Carmel? I attempt to explain that this unique building is the world headquarters of an Islamic-related religious group called *Baha'i*. Some of the people comment that it is rather ironic that Baha'i, whose original ties are with Islam, should have its world headquarters in Haifa.

We have already mentioned that Baha'i has its roots in the Shiite wing of Islam. According to the Shiites, Muhammad gave authority to Ali, his son-in-law. Ali passed the authority on to twelve successive leaders or Imams. The last of the Imams disappeared in A.D. 874. The Shiite Muslims look forward to his return at a time of great world need.[55]

The new Baha'i faith arose from this Islamic background. In 1844, a young Sufi in Persia (Iran) claimed that he was the Bab (door) to announce the coming of the twelfth Imam or manifestation of god for this age. Like John the Baptist, he was a forerunner. In 1850 Bab was martyred. In 1863, one of Bab's followers, Baha'u'llah, proclaimed that he was the one, the manifestation of god, whose coming had been announced by Bab.[56]

From such Islamic and Sufi roots and traditions, a new faith was formed. According to the Baha'is, the Bab and his follower, Baha'u'llah, are co-founders of Baha'i. Baha'u'llah is seen as the final culmination of god's revelation to man for this age. Earlier manifestations of god such as Krishna, Buddha, Zoroaster, Moses, Jesus, and Muhammad spoke the message needed in their time. Baha'u'llah is seen by the Baha'is as the final revelation needed for the present era for all mankind.[57] In fact, the promised second coming of Christ has taken place in the life of Baha'u'llah, according to Baha'i teaching.[58]

In a strict sense, Baha'i is not a New Consciousness group. The chief emphases of Baha'i include the oneness of all great world religions, harmony, universal brotherhood, and world order. Baha'i meetings are characterized by a quiet, verbal manner with an emphasis on social problems rather than mystical experience. In the West, Baha'i has lost most of the Sufi mystical qualities which it had in the beginning.[59]

PART FOUR
Western Secular New Consciousness Groups

THREE MAIN STREAMS OF NEW CONSCIOUSNESS

The New Consciousness (hereafter N.C.) revolution can be seen as having three main emphases. One emphasis, as we have seen, is to update ancient Far Eastern and Middle Eastern traditions for Western consumption. The Hindu-related, Buddhist-related, and Islamic-related groups are in this category. In our study, we have discussed some modern Western groups that have been influenced in definite ways by these ancient traditions.

A second emphasis is found among the groups which attempt to recover consciousness paths which they believe are buried in the Western tradition but are half-forgotten. Examples of this category are the neopagan, ceremonial magic, and witchcraft groups.

The third emphasis is found among those groups which are modern Western attempts to work out a N.C. path. Some of them owe debts to the East or to the remote past. In the main, however, they have behind them a Western and modern individual who has walked on the streets of Western cities and traveled in automobiles and planes.[1]

THE VASTNESS OF THE WESTERN SECULAR STREAM

The third category is a vast field. One popular book on the N.C. movements states that there are more than eight thousand ways to "awaken in North America." [2]

We will look at three representative and somewhat dramatic examples of the Western secular N.C. groups: Scientology, Silva Mind Control, and est. Scientology is a rather unique case. In the beginning it claimed to be a scientific or psychoanalytic group. For various reasons it now calls itself a religion. Critics see it as a pseudoscience movement rooted in the world of the occult and science fiction.[3]

1
Scientology (L. Ron Hubbard)

In recent years I was a guest at the well-known Fort Harrison Hotel in the resort area of Clearwater, Florida. The hotel was a downtown landmark and the pride of the city. In a sudden and mysterious manner the hotel was purchased, in 1976, with money from the Western European country of Luxembourg. Two hundred tight-lipped strangers moved in. To the dismay of many Clearwater citizens, the purchaser was the rich Church of Scientology. Scientology leaders announced that the hotel was to become the movement's "Flag Land Base" for the advanced training of the international elite. These trainees would be chosen from Scientology's reported five million members. The founder of Scientology, L. Ron Hubbard, came to Clearwater to inaugurate the program.[4]

What is Scientology? Who is L. Ron Hubbard? What is its place in the N.C. world?

THE LIFE OF L. RON HUBBARD AND THE DEVELOPMENTS OF SCIENTOLOGY

Lafayette Ronald Hubbard (affectionately known as Elron by his followers) is the founder and central figure of Scientology. A familiarity with Hubbard's life is necessary for an understanding of the development of Scientology. In recent years he has preferred to live outside the public eye, cruising the Mediterranean on his thirty-three hundred ton yacht, *Apollo*. In 1968 he announced that his work was ended and that, "Now it is up to others." [5] Since that time, however, he has continued to add to his already over "ten million words" about Scientology. He stays in instant communication with Scientology headquarters at Saint Hill Manor in England by means of a special Telex typewriter on board his yacht.

The veneration of Hubbard. To Scientology groups all over the world Hubbard is something more than a founder and leader. *Christianity Today* magazine states that the veneration of Hubbard by Scientologists approaches the veneration of Jesus Christ by Christians. Pictures of him and quotations from his writings adorn the walls of Scientology meeting places. A sculptured bust of Hubbard is usually displayed at the front of their lecture halls. Oftentimes services begin with the lowering of lights, a focusing of a spotlight on Hubbard's bust, and a recorded message from

Hubbard. Hubbard is evidently considered infallible in matters of Scientology belief and practice.[6]

Hubbard's questionable record. Much has been said about Scientology's founder and leader. Their literature frequently refers to Hubbard as an engineer, mathematician, and nuclear physicist. *Who's Who in the Southwest* credits him with an engineering degree from George Washington University. George Washington University denies ever having granted Hubbard a degree, affirming only that he dropped out his second year after flunking physics and being placed on probation.[7]

Hubbard also used to tag a Ph.D. to his name, which he claimed he acquired from Sequoia University. *Nation* magazine points out that "this institution, now defunct, was headed by Dr. Joseph Hough, a chiropractor, who refused to testify before a California assembly subcommittee looking into reports that some colleges in the state sold graduate degrees for profit." [8] At any rate, Sequoia's degrees are not recognized by any accredited college or university. So much criticism arose over his bogus degree that Hubbard renounced its use in 1966. In order to save face, he said the degree was given up to protest the damage being done by psychiatrists and nuclear physicists who called themselves doctor.[9]

L. Ron Hubbard was born in Nebraska in 1911, the son of a career officer in the United States Navy. His claim that his grandfather "owned a quarter of Montana" is denied by Hubbard's son. During the late twenties his father's navy duty took his family to the Far East. There were long spells of duty in China and Japan. Here young Ron was exposed to a number of the Eastern influences that helped shape his emerging philosophy. He claims that he started formulating Scientology at the age of twelve. One easily recognized influence on Hubbard was a navy doctor who filled the young boy's mind with Freudian ideas during his early years.

Science fiction background. Hubbard returned to the United States in 1930 for his short career in college. After college, Hubbard led several scientific expeditions into the primitive jungles of Central America and at the age of twenty-five was initiated into the exclusive Explorers' Club of New York. It was during this period that he began writing, mostly science fiction, and was called to Hollywood to write several scenarios. In 1938 he finished the manuscript of a book called *Excalibur*, containing some of the imaginative and futuristic ideas that he later amplified into the concepts of Dianetics and Scientology.

The life of Hubbard has a pattern which is remarkably like that of ancient and medieval shamans or cult leaders. He had an unusual childhood, wide travel, and a power-of-imagination world view. As we shall see, he reports that while he was in the navy he was twice pronounced dead but was rescued to help save mankind.

In Hubbard's case, the initial vehicle for his ideas was science fiction. Many critics speak of Scientology as the first science fiction religion. It is true that Hubbard's movement plays with themes and terminology of the science fiction world in a new and unique way.[10]

After five years of naval service during World War II, Hubbard became critically ill. Crippled, blind, and twice declared dead by doctors, he rebounded to perfect health. This recovery, he affirms, came about by applying the principles later described in his book *Dianetics: The Modern Science of Mental Health*. It was during this period, between 1947 and 1950, that he worked on his theories. Then in May, 1950, they were previewed in an issue of *Astounding Science Fiction. Dianetics: The Modern Science of Mental Health* was completed in the space of sixty days that same year and sold one hundred thousand copies within three months of its publication. It should be noted that the professional journals of psychology, psychiatry, and medicine all ignored it. *The Saturday Evening Post* explains its popularity this way:

> Dianetics was enough like psychoanalysis to impress a good many people, and also had the advantage that anyone who bought Hubbard's book, could play doctor at home, without all those tedious years in medical school. In no time hundreds of thousands of Americans, armed with Hubbard's book, were playing Sigmund Freud for each other.[11]

The popularity of the book soon faded and it dropped from the best-selling charts, but Dianetics had planted the seed for the cult of Scientology.

Scientology as a religion. Scientology arose from the ashes of Dianetics in 1952 with several new developments. The name was changed and the movement was now presented to the public as a religion instead of a science. The meeting places formerly called orgs were now chartered as churches.

This decision to change to a religion came as no surprise to Sam Moscowitz, a science fiction editor and fellow author. "Three years earlier," he recalls, "Hubbard spoke before the Eastern Science Fiction Association in Newark, New Jersey. I don't recall his exact words. But in effect, he told us that writing science fiction for about a penny a word was no way to make a living. If you really want to make a million, he said, the quickest way is to start your own religion." [12]

The change from a professed science to a religion was almost forced upon Hubbard. The New Jersey Board of Medical Examiners charged Hubbard with operating an unlicensed medical school. He gave out M.D.

degrees. He said the degree meant "Master of Dianetics," not doctor of medicine.[13] The prominent psychiatrist, William Menninger, denounced Dianetic counseling as potentially dangerous. The Manhattan endocrinologist who wrote the laudatory foreword to Dianetics broke with Hubbard, charging that Hubbard was heading toward absolutism and authoritarianism.[14] Hubbard was also involved in a court case connected with the abduction of his own son and another court procedure to shed his second wife, who termed him "hopelessly insane."[15]

In Australia, Scientology was banned. For a number of years England has refused to give foreign Scientology students visas to enter the country to study Scientology as a religion. In this case Hubbard claims his school is an educational institution. When the scientific claims of Scientology are challenged, Hubbard reaffirms that it is a religion.

In spite of his difficulties, Hubbard continues to write extensively for Scientology. In 1966 there was an attack by the United States Internal Revenue Service on the tax-free status of the Founding Church of Scientology in Washington D.C. Hubbard resigned all church directorships and received a fee of two hundred thousand dollars for the use of his name. He boasted to his friends that he had seven million dollars stashed away in his Swiss bank accounts.[16]

BASIC TEACHINGS OF SCIENTOLOGY

Dianetics—the scientific phase. L. Ron Hubbard's ideas first gained prominence with the publication of his famous book, *Dianetics*, in 1950. The book was an immediate sensation. Excerpts published in a science fiction magazine brought in thousands of letters.

Engrams Cause all our Problems. In this book, Hubbard declares that the mind controls the brain. The mind itself has two parts, the analytic and the reactive. The analytic part is similar to Freud's conscious mind. The reactive part is similar to the unconscious. The analytic mind, unless upset, works with precision. Experiences of shock cause engrams (sensory impressions of the event) to be recorded in the reactive or unconscious mind. These records cause mental and mind-body troubles until they are dislodged.[17]

Most neuroses, psychoses, and some illnesses are caused by the engrams which are stored in the reactive mind. Some engrams are produced while the child is still in the womb by such things as a husband beating his pregnant wife. Other engrams are stored in a baby by thumps, kicks, or violent sexual intercourse. The mother's constipation or sneezing could cause engrams in the unborn baby. One person was told that he was a kleptomaniac because his father beat his mother during pregnancy, shouting, "Take that! Take it, I tell you!" These commands resulted in the baby growing up to be a compulsive stealer.[18]

Engrams can be removed! Hubbard and Dianetics have come to the rescue. The patient (called a preclear) can come to a Hubbard-trained therapist called an auditor. The auditor uses special techniques (commands and questions) to help the patient in looking for forgotten shock incidents. This interview is sometimes called Dianetic Reverie. Patients are guided through auto accidents; war injuries; operations; beatings by drunken fathers; falls from the crib; the birth trauma; and back into prenatals, such as attempted abortion; looking for the dreaded engrams.[19]

When the patient has confronted and relived the engram (shock memory), the the engram is pushed out of the reactive mind. It is at this point that sinus problems disappear, backaches vanish, and stuttering miraculously improves. As a result of engram removal, bad eyesight is corrected and the common cold cured. The preclear is on his way to being "clear."[20]

Obviously this Dianetic system had weaknesses and was shallow. But in the early months of the movement, literally hundreds of thousands of people—many of them well-educated and intelligent—were drawn into Dianetics. Hubbard became nationally prominent. *Dianetics* sold over a million copies. Dianetic Research Centers were established across the United States. Prominent scientists and medical doctors gave testimony as to the value of this new therapy.[21]

It was not long before troubles began. Clears were theoretically people without neuroses or problems. But few, if any, clears were produced. Financial and organizational mismanagement in the Dianetic movement was evident. Early medical and scientific followers felt that Hubbard was moving beyond the sober scientific approach into the realm of the supernatural and the occult.[22]

Scientology—The Supernatural or Occult Phase.

A. The Thetans

Dianetics was primarily secular in its emphases. Hubbard's continuing research led him to teach the existence of the soul or the Thetan. In *Scientology: The Fundamentals of Thought* Hubbard states that his greatest contribution to mankind was the isolation, description, and handling of the Thetan. This new truth was discovered, he said, in Phoenix, Arizona, in 1951.

You were once a god. Your Thetan is the real you as over against the body, mind, physical universe, or anything else. It is nonphysical and immortal. It has always lived. At your core, you are a fallen immortal god or Thetan. When the Thetan enters your body it brings with it all the engrams of millions of years of previous existence. Thetans are reincarnated over trillions of years. This means that you must clear out or erase the engrams of the past, re-die dramatic deaths you experienced in sinking ocean liners or shocks you experienced from falling off the wooden horse of Troy. One patient traced his persistent headaches to a blow he had received as a Roman centurion in 215 B.C.[23]

In earlier days, the goal of Hubbard's movement was to get followers clear of the engrams of this life. The new goal is to seek to whisk away the engrams of a million previous lifetimes. If you achieve this new goal, you will be an Operating Thetan. Such a status means you are free of the shackles of this universe and have almost miraculous powers.[24]

B. The Enslavement of the Thetans (the Real Secret of the Universe)

Your former life as a god. Hubbard's science fiction background must have helped him in explaining the background of the Thetans in his book *History of Man.* According to Hubbard, ultimate reality was originally populated by the Thetans. These Thetans were eternal, uncreated, omnipotent, and omniscient. They were personal beings, free from all laws and all cause-effect relationships.

Despite their exalted state, the Thetans were bored. To entertain themselves, they began creating universes about thirty-five billion years ago and played with these universes, which were external to themselves. Even this type of play was boring.

Your fall from godhood. Next, the Thetans voluntarily handicapped themselves and limited their powers of knowledge. After millions of years, the lure of the universe which the Thetans had created out of matter, energy, space, and time (MEST) snared them. They became trapped in the material universe which they had created. The Thetans found themselves incarnated as the plants and other life forms. They kept on reincarnating as the plants and animals died. By the time evolution had ascended to man, the incarnate Thetans had descended into forgetfulness. Thetans in humans have forgotten their innate and rightful deity. They think they are bodies.[25]

Many human religions, especially those of the Far East, have taught the innate divinity of man. Many of these religions have told of avatars or incarnations of god who would help us recover our deity and find freedom and release. But L. Ron Hubbard states that he alone has discovered the spiritual technology that all other religious leaders have always needed. He alone knows the way to help man recover his heritage as a free and immortal player or god.

Discovering your problem. In the *History of Man* Hubbard describes some of the shock encounters in Thetan's past. Auditors use his book to help a preclear to find out if he has an engram from one of these early stages. The stages of man's development are outlined in *History of Man*. If you are upset at the mention of a clam, for example, this means that you had a shock experience when you were a clam. If you have trouble with crying, your water ducts were probably clogged by sand when you were once a primordial clam. When you were a sloth, you often fell out of trees. This caused engrams to form in your reactive mind. The Piltdown Man stage had many men eating their wives. This obviously caused engrams.[26]

At death, you as a theta leave the body and go to the between-lives place. You report in and are given a forgetter implant. The report area for most Thetans is Mars. Then you are shot down to another body just before it is born.[27]

For sixty trillion years you have undergone shocks and accumulated engrams as a Thetan in repeated reincarnations. Scientology has a big clearing job to do.

C. *The E-meter*, Clear State, and the Operating Thetan.

Tin cans and your condition. An important new Scientology development in the early 1950s was the adoption of a device for liberating the enslaved Thetan of his engrams. This device, called an E-meter, is an electrical instrument which measures the resistance of an object to electric current.[28]

As a preclear with engram trouble, you hold a tin can in each hand. The cans are attached to the dial of the machine. The machine passes a small but harmless amount of electricity through the tin cans. The auditor asks you questions about troublesome areas. If the question asked arouses emotion in you the needle will fluctuate. It is a galvanic skin response. If it is a heavy response it is called "Rock-slam." You then bring the engram shock of a past experience of your life out in the open. When the needle stops you are clear of this particular engram.[29]

Eventually, after the expenditure of much money and time, you can become clear. Few individuals can reach clear without the expenditure of a thousand dollars. And there are a number of stages beyond clear. Some pay as much as fifteen thousand dollars for higher levels of liberation.

Becoming god again. The ultimate goal beyond clear is to become an Operating Thetan or O.T. It obviously takes a committed Scientologist to locate within himself and dissolve engrams that are billions of years old. But it is worth it according to Scientology. As an O.T., you are independent of all the problems of MEST (Matter-Energy-Space-Time). As an O.T., you can even have "out of body" experiences, practice clairvoyance (see beyond the bounds of normal vision), and feel that you encompass the entire universe. Since your Thetan or self is not your mind or body you can operate above the level of thought and understand intuitively. The primordial deity within you is recovered when you regain total thetanhood.[30]

Above all, as an Operating Thetan, you can once again (as did the original Thetans) create matter, space, and time, the substance of our universe. As a Thetan you can make things go right. You can help purify individuals of negative emotions, evil spirits, and overts (harmful actions), and withholds (moral transgressions). People who are against Scientology, especially former church members, reinforce these negatives. So any Scientologist who harasses a declared suppressive person is helping that person progress toward final freedom.[31]

It is important to note that some of the emphases of Scientology have been adapted by Werner Erhard into the est theory. We will note these similarities in our study of est.

D. Scientology and N.C.

The influence of the East. It is obvious from our study that the recent developments in Scientology are similar to many of the ancient Hindu and Buddhist concepts of reality. The ultimate nature of reality is in the Thetan, or mind, or consciousness. Mind, ideas, and spirit are prior to and more important than MEST (matter, energy, space, time). The MEST world is similar to the Hindu idea of the material world as maya or ultimately illusory. Hindu concepts such as karma and reincarnation are also evident in Scientology.[32]

The whole purpose of Scientology is to pass candidates through its grades, self-discoveries, and breakthroughs to the ultimate recovery of uninhibited spiritual oneness. Even if you begin on a mundane level, the ultimate goal is mystical in nature. Perhaps the uniqueness of Scientology is its outlining of techniques by which you go from mundane to the mystical. In Scientology everything is catalogued and precisely defined. Scientology combines modern psychological terms, science fiction concepts, Eastern religious teachings, and basic occult ideas.[33]

The whole process outlined in Scientology is supposed to teach you to play and be liberated like the Thetans before they were enslaved many billions of years ago. The process is supposed to be challenging and delightful. Scientology is similar to some of the ancient consciousness groups with the difference that it utilizes twentieth-century language.[34]

Scientology spawns many groups. Scientology continues to prove attractive to millions of people. Many ambitious people, seeing the success of Scientology, have borrowed fragments of its philosophy and technology to help them form their own groups. Werner Erhard's est, for example,

69190

has combined significant tenets of Scientology with other complex spiritual-psychological traditions. Other groups have been founded by former leaders in Scientology. Charles Berner, after ten years in Scientology, formed Abilitism. Berner borrowed techniques from Scientology but claims that his group is oriented toward a more flexible, open, and love-centered kind of release.[35]

CONTINUING DEVELOPMENTS IN SCIENTOLOGY

Scientology is an ever-changing and still growing group or church. The following events are representative of its adaptability.

A. In 1966 the tax-free status of the Founding Church of Scientology in Washington, D.C., was questioned. To help the situation Hubbard resigned all church directorships. Before this Hubbard had received ten percent of all revenues.

B. In 1969 Hubbard defined the purpose of the Scientology Church in a statement utilizing overt religious terminology. The mission of Scientology, he said, is to help a person become aware of himself as an immortal being. Scientology wants to erase a person's sin so that he can be good enough to recognize God.[36]

C. In recent years Scientology has promoted programs related to social concern. These programs involve drug abuse, alcoholism, and mental retardation.[37]

D. In 1971, after a difficult federal court battle, Scientology was recognized again in the United States as a religion and was given constitutional guarantees. Australia and Britain also modified their opposition to Scientology.[38]

E. In the early 1970s Scientology mounted an offensive against book, magazine, and newspaper publishers who printed attacks on the church. In 1970-72 more than one hundred libel suits were filed against such varied critics as the American Medical Association, the National Education Association, and the Washington *Post*.[39]

F. At the same time it was suing critics, Scientology tried to introduce some reforms of policies that were being criticized.

As late as 1976, however, the California Superior Court ruled that Scientology was still following the fair game policy. In relation to a defected Scientology official, the court said that the Scientologists were lying, suing, and atempting to destroy this former executive.

In 1977, Federal prosecutors brought Scientology officials before a Washington, D.C., grand jury. The Scientologists were charged with infiltrating the Justice Department and the Internal Revenue service and

91

stealing confidential documents.[40]

In 1969, a United States Federal Court said that Scientology had successfully made out a case proving that it was a genuine religion. As we remember, in 1952 Hubbard had organized Dianetics for the practice of science. Beginning as early as 1954 Hubbard moved from a scientific to a religious emphasis. Since then the symbolism of Scientology has become increasingly ecclesiastical. Ordained ministers of the Church of Scientology wear clerical collars and pectoral crosses. The church holds informal Sunday services with liturgies. There is a liturgical manual published for christenings, weddings, and funerals.[41]

The meeting places of Scientology are called missions or churches. In some cases the auditing session of Scientology is called the confessional. It is obvious that Scientology is making a serious bid to become a significant religious movement. In fact, it continues to claim to be the fulfillment and culmination of all religions.[42]

THE ORGANIZATION AND GROWTH OF SCIENTOLOGY

Although Hubbard resigned all church directorships in 1966, he still exerts a dominant influence on the church and its development. World headquarters of Scientology shift in location. In recent years the world headquarters has been in Los Angeles. Membership is claimed as more than five million throughout the world. More than three million members are said to live in the United States. These figures are doubtless exaggerated but Scientology is alive and flourishing. There are twenty-two major Scientology churches or area centers and some one hundred missions.

A major advanced training center is located aboard the thirty-three hundred ton yacht *Apollo*, the roving residence of Hubbard. The *Apollo* is one of seven crafts which cruise the Mediterranean and adjacent areas, and constitute the Sea Org, a community of dedicated Scientologists. (*Org* is the Scientologists' word for a group.) [43]

Every day bulletins, pamphlets, books, and tapes go out from the *Apollo* to some eighty-five United States franchises (centers for introductory training) and fourteen orgs (centers for advanced training). Centers and orgs are also found on most of the other continents of the world. Ireland is being considered as a new land base for Hubbard.[44]

In 1976 a hotel and bank building in Clearwater, Florida, were purchased to be used for advanced training for international elite. In 1976 cash was paid for buildings in Los Angeles, Boston, New York City, Saint Louis, Washington, D.C., Miami, San Diego, and Riverside, California.[45]

SCIENTOLOGY'S OUTREACH AND RECRUITING METHODS

Who Joins? What type of people does Scientology attract? It seems to be attracting all kinds, from hippies, drawn by its radical departure from tradition, to engineers and computer programmers, entertainment personalities, and even Protestant clergy. *Parents* magazine states that many followers are high school graduates; "intrigued with the trappings of science, they are vulnerable to pseudo-science." [46] Still others come into Scientology who are lonely, weak, confused, and emotionally ill.[47]

Scientology has recently given considerable attention to artists, musicians, and theatrical people. Celebrity centers have been established in key cities. Creativity is said to be a part of the total freedom which Scientology releases.[48]

Not only does Scientology attract people from every walk of life but also it attracts people for a diversity of reasons. Scientology holds a special attraction for those who are in trouble. Many who join are disillusioned with society or religion. Others come on the promise that Scientology offers health, happiness, and superintelligence. Many come because they are offered the opportunity to pour out their thoughts and problems to someone who will listen. One study notes that recruits to Scientology are often young, intelligent, and idealistic. They become fanatics on the subject, almost impervious to argument, and are quick to cut themselves off from doubters.[49]

How people are reached. One of the keys to understanding the growth and success of Scientology is to examine its methods of recruitment. The *Economist* speaks of Scientology as doing "a remarkable marketing job." [50] Three main methods are employed by the group to bring in new prospects. The first method is by word of mouth. The process of auditing requires a great deal of time, so many followers leave their secular jobs and join the staffs of Scientology, working to pay their way through processing. They become auditors, calling themselves ministers, and are instructed in the fine art of beating the bushes for customers. Some of the techniques included are:

—"I will talk to anyone." Auditors are instructed to place newspaper ads saying that "Reverend" So-and-so will talk to anyone about anything. When calls are received, the minister assures the caller that his problems are indeed significant and that he should visit the church. When the caller arrives, he is given the pitch on Scientology processing.

—"Illness Researchers." Scientology disciples place newspaper ads asking victims of polio and other crippling diseases to volunteer for examination by a "research foundation" or "charitable organization." When a person responds, he is told "that there is a way (via Scientology) to improve his ability to walk or breathe or whatever."

—"Casualty Contact." Under this heading, the ministers are instructed in the techniques of the ghoul. They are to follow accident stories and death notices in newspapers, note the names of families involved, and contact them, "express compassion and concern," and try to get the persons to come to the Scientology church.[51]

Another effective technique of drawing people into the fold has been the use of literature promising health, new ability, intelligence, and a better life. What human being on earth does not desire these things? If you will read Hubbard's introductory book *Scientology: The Fundamentals of Thought,* you can see how readers can be taken in by the pseudoscientific terminology, the grand claims and promises, and the generalities which seem to exclude no one. One such statement in Hubbard's book says:

It is the only science or study known which is capable of uniformly producing marked and significant increases in intelligence and general ability. Scientology processing among other things can improve the intelligence quotient of an individual, his ability or desire to communicate, his social attitudes, his capability and domestic harmony, his fertility, his artistic creativity, his reaction time and his health.[52]

In recent years airplanes have been used to fly over football crowds towing streamers proclaiming slogans such as, "Scientology makes the Able Man more Able." Advertisements are slipped under car windshield wipers, placed under apartment house doorways, and posted on utility poles.

Testimonies of actors and sports stars are used. One man said that he was attracted to Scientology because of pro quarterback John Brodie's testimonial that Scientology healed his throwing arm.[53]

The third major method of recruitment involves the free introductory lectures. I well remember my first contact with Scientology. I was in the Los Angeles area for a week's speaking engagement. Near my hotel was an attractive Scientology storefront center. I walked in and was invited to attend a demonstration. An attractive young woman pointed out by means of an evaluative test and some charts that my life could be happier and more successful through Scientology. For only fifteen or twenty dollars, she said, I could take a communication course which would start me on this new and more glorious life.

Beyond the four day communication course are other courses. A higher course is called Grade I. In Grade I you are taught to recognize the source of your problems and make them vanish. Grade III will release you from all upsets of the past. In Grade IV new abilities are released. By the time you reach Grade VII you are close to clear. At this level you can start taking an auditor's course and thereby begin to earn money to pay for more advanced training. Once you become clear you can start working toward becoming an Operating Thetan. It may cost as much as fifteen thousand dollars for total freedom and complete happiness.[54]

SECULAR EVALUATION OF SCIENTOLOGY

Hubbard claims that tens of thousands of successful case histories (attested before public officials) are on file in Scientology organizations.[55] On the other hand, much has been written in an attempt to discredit Scientology based on the testimony of many disillusioned dropouts.[56] Scientology is seen as harmful in three major secular areas: psychological, social, and medical. As we shall see, it also has serious theological weaknesses from the biblical perspective.

Psychological criticism. Psychologists and psychiatrists have reacted in a negative manner to Scientology because it rejects and even criticizes psychiatry and other scientifically endorsed approaches to mental health problems. One Scientology official has been quoted as saying, "A Dianetic auditor can do more permanent good for a person than every psychologist and psychiatrist in the world wrapped up together." [57]

More important is the accusation by many psychologists who claim that auditing can endanger a person's mental health. For example, say the psychologists, instead of discussing present reality, the auditor tries to push the preclear into a world of fantasy. Under the sway of the auditor's will and the apparently scientific verdict of the E-meter, a preclear will usually accept the auditor's statement that he is suppressing something, even if he cannot remember anything. Sooner or later the preclear will begin to exhibit symptoms resembling those of schizophrenia. These symptoms are usually encouraged. The preclear is told that the hallucinations he is experiencing are in reality factual incidents of the Thetan's past. According to Scientology teaching the discovery of these engrams is the high road to health and freedom.[58]

The Anderson Commission report, made to the Parliament of Australia, called Scientology "The world's largest organization of unqualified persons engaged in the practice of dangerous techniques which masquerade as mental therapy."

Social criticism. Scientology has been judged socially harmful because for many years it has advised its members to disconnect, or to discontinue association from critics of the cult or what are called suppressing forces. Many followers actually sever all relationships with their families. Processing controls the thought of followers and introduces negative information about loved ones. Such estrangements can be deep and lasting, oftentimes leaving heartsick parents no longer able to speak rationally with their children.

Christianity Today points out that through the utilization of interior group loyalty and exterior rejection, Scientologists have developed the self-image of a persecuted messiah sect. This approach results in hostility toward those who find fault with their beliefs and practices.[59]

Although, as we have seen, Scientology has recently announced some social concern, its major emphasis continues to be on self-improvement or self-mastery. It is quite expensive and its benefits are obviously unavailable for the poor. Little is said about the plight of the homeless and the oppressed.[60] In fact, some charge Scientology with reducing its followers to working slaves. They must work in the movement to pay the high price to become a clear or an Operating Thetan. This can often take energy, time, and money for long years. In fact, young people have spent an entire year's college funds within a matter of weeks on Scientology courses. Careers are abandoned and jobs lost as young people seek to be clear. This is called Scientology addiction.[61]

Medical criticism. According to Hubbard, 70 percent of our illnesses are mentally induced, including such diseases as arthritis, asthma, rheumatism, and heart trouble. The subtle deception of Scientology is that there may be just enough truth to this claim to make it work in some cases. The inherent danger in this approach is that the afflicted person may abandon professional medical treatment in favor of Scientology and thus expose himself to the possibility of disastrous physical consequences.[62] In all fairness, physical healing has been downplayed by Scientology in recent years.

THEOLOGICAL CRITICISM

As a religion, Scientology is obviously different from the classical Christian view. It draws from many religions but perhaps the strongest influence is from Hinayana or Southern Buddhism.

Like classical Eastern thought, essential man is seen as innately divine and basically good. Through Scientology techniques inherent divinity can be recovered. The good news of God in Christ coming to man's rescue is irrelevant and unnecessary from the Scientology perspective. Man is naturally immortal and will live on in countless reincarnations.

As we have seen, there is no ultimate standard for right or wrong beyond the cause of upholding and advancing Scientology. Evil is primarily related to anyone misusing or degrading Scientology.[63]

LESSONS TO BE LEARNED FROM SCIENTOLOGY

It is easy enough to criticize some of the almost unbelievable teachings of Scientology. From the success of Scientology, however, certain lessons can be learned by evangelical Christians. Among lessons that come readily to mind are:

A. The importance of developing skills in communication in the area of religion.

B. The importance of giving people undivided personal attention.

C. The desire of people to find an answer to ultimate questions such as, Why are we here? and Where are we going? in clear-cut and understandable form.

D. The desire of people to deal constructively with personal failings and their past.

Despite its obvious weaknesses and inconsistencies, Scientology is making a strong bid to become a serious religious movement in this era.[64]

2
Silva Mind Control and est—Experience-oriented Western Secular New Consciousness Groups

Hindu, Buddhist, and Islamic consciousness techniques have been updated and packaged for Western consumption. Transcendental Meditation, Nicheren Shoshu, and Subud, which we have discussed, are examples of these Far Eastern and Middle Eastern updates.

Scientology is of the West, but with its science fiction relationship it is a movement distinctive unto itself.

Silva Mind Control and Werner Erhard's est, although influenced by the East, are decidedly Western in tone and style. Both Silva Mind Control and est have ties with the human potential movement which began with sensitivity training in the late 1940s. By the 1970s there was a growing emphasis in the human potential movement on transpersonal experience. *Transpersonal* is a recently-coined term and refers to both mystical experiences and parapsychological events.[65]

The latest trend in the human potential field is the development of large scale N.C. organizations. These new movements present an assortment of consciousness techniques in ready-made packages under an incorporated name. Examples of such developments are Silva Mind Control, est, T.M., and Arica. These groups and their offshoots have nearly doubled in size each year since 1970.

Economy, uniformity, and publicity attend the packaged approach. Some N.C. types who travel on their own are critical of these charter trips with standardized fees and overzealous travelers.[66]

Contemporary Western N.C. programs can be divided into two types. One type deals with techniques which seek to modify and control, through the will or volition, a person's own mental, emotional, and physiological states. This type does not use hypnotic programming by another person. Any reference to psychic power is secondary to self-mastery.

A second type of program constitutes an approach which is criticized by many psychologists and psychiatrists. These critics say that this second type seeks to develop psychic powers through hypnosis. The groups attacked deny that hypnosis is used. Instead of hypnosis, the groups prefer to use terms such as *programming, Alpha training,* and *conditioning.*

3
Silva Mind Control (SMC)

Would you like to live more happily, more effectively, here and now? Would you like to turn your tensions into creative energy, grow on the level with the gurus, mock migraine headaches, and stop smoking? What about developing the ability to tune in on thoughts of faraway people or help heal distant loved ones who are ill? [67]

All of this and much more is promised if you will take a forty-eight-hour course in Silva Mind Control (SMC). SMC may be the world's fastest growing N.C. group which has its origin in the West. At least it is one of the world's most practical consciousness groups. It has borrowed freely from both Eastern and Western sources, but the end product is as American as apple pie.[68]

THE ORIGIN AND DEVELOPMENT OF SILVA MIND CONTROL

Some people stumble over the fact that SMC is the creation of an uneducated (in a formal sense), plain, Mexican-American, José Silva. His life constitutes a modern Horatio Alger story.

Silva was born in the dusty border town of Laredo, Texas, in 1914. His father died when he was four. At six he became the family breadwinner. Self-educated, he learned electronics by mail order and opened up a radio repair shop. This work and a television addition became the financial support of his twenty-six years of research in mind control. He claims to have put 1.5 million dollars of his own money into the development of SMC.

During his five years in the military, Silva's interest in psychology was aroused by what he thought were idiotic induction questions. The regimental psychiatrist allowed Silva to pursue his psychological interests by using his library. Silva became particularly interested in studying hypnosis and parapsychology.[69]

Returning home at the end of World War II, Silva used his hypnosis research to help his ten children improve their learning ability. He had read about the Alpha level of the brain wave cycles. The Alpha level constitutes a lower level of activity than the more normal Beta level. Using hypnosis, he brought his children's minds to the lower frequency level of Alpha. At the Alpha level he discovered that the brain received and stored more information. The children's school records improved.

Silva's research continued. He next developed some exercises that would bring the brain to the relaxed Alpha level yet keep it more alert than in hypnosis. These exercises called for relaxed concentration and vivid mental visualization. The children's grades went up sharply upon using these new techniques.[70]

There was to be another discovery. To his amazement, Silva discovered, in 1953, that he had taught his daughter to read his mind and anticipate his questions. He had stumbled into a way to arouse latent extrasensory and psychic power. Over the next ten years, 1953-1963, Silva trained thirty-nine Laredo children to use ESP.[71]

Within another three years Silva had developed the basic Mind Control course which is now used around the world. In 1963 formal Mind Control classes were started in Mexico. Word began to get out to the English-speaking public beyond Laredo. In 1966, Dr. N. E. West, psychologist at Wayland Baptist College in Plainview, Texas, invited Silva to lecture to his students. The students spread the word about Silva's method in West Texas. Silva's first paying course was held in Amarillo, Texas. A group of eighty-six people paid him thirty-five dollars each to conduct a twelve-hour seminar in Mind Control.[72]

The long years of research were primarily financed by Silva's electronics business. Silva has lived to see the fruit of his work. Today the Mind Control organization is worldwide in its outreach.

THE METHODS AND TEACHINGS OF SILVA MIND CONTROL

The basic course of Silva Mind Control involves four days for a period of twelve hours each day. After introductory lectures, students are taught to meditate. No drugs or biofeedback machines are used. In the beginning Silva did not have the money for the biofeedback machines. In a thirty-minute meditation exercise students are led into the Alpha level.[73]

Medical scientists have established that the brain emits electrical impulses associated with different states of consciousness. These impulses are classified into four brain-wave patterns that can be recorded by a biofeedback machine (called an EEG machine). The rhythms of this energy are measured in cycles per second (CPS).

Alpha level and spectacular results. The majority of people, during waking hours, function on the Beta wave (fourteen to thirty-two cycles per second). This is the outer consciousness level associated with physical activity, work routines, anxiety, tension or anger.

The Alpha level (seven to fourteen cycles per second) is called the inner consciousness level. It is associated with creativity, inspiration, tranquility, learning, memory ideas, and concentration. When you are daydreaming or just going to sleep, or just awakening you are usually in Alpha. The Theta level (four to seven cycles per second) is a sleep level. It relates to deeper levels of meditation, recall, and learning capabilities.

The Delta level (four cps and below) is the unconscious or deep sleep level.

The heart of SMC is that it can teach you to use the Alpha level and achieve dynamic and even spectacular results. Silva Mind Control can help you to relax. But it claims more. Through its techniques, your psychic powers can be awakened.

In recent publications, Silva spells out in practical form how to reach the Alpha level and then outlines Alpha level possibilities. To bring you to the Alpha level, such devices as spot gazing, visualization, and numerical countdown are suggested. Dynamic meditation involves visualizing problems on your mental screen and then visualizing the solutions or at least a happy scene related to a solution.[74]

Memory techniques utilizing memory pegs and the Three Finger triggering mechanism are illustrated. For speed learning, the reading of material into a recorder is utilized. The material is to be played back to you after you have gone down to the Alpha level.[75]

Creative use of sleep. For Silva, sleep can be creative. In a dream, Silva contends he was given the winning number of the Mexican lottery. Through programming Silva suggests that you can remember a dream. In Alpha, before going to sleep, review a serious problem and state in a specific way that you want information to solve it. An answer will probably be forthcoming when you awaken.[76]

Words have power for Silva Mind Control. Concentrating and repeating a thought helps make the thought become true because our bodies will transform the thought into action. This power of repetition is greatly amplified at Alpha and Theta levels.[77]

Visualizing and the loss of fat. One of the most dramatic emphases of SMC is the power of imagination. For fatness, visualize on the Alpha level the reducing foods and yourself as thin and handsome. Similar mental screening is suggested to eliminate the smoking habit. Go into the Alpha state in emergencies and stop bleeding by visualizing the pain area as free of bleeding. Reports are given by SMC graduates of the cure of astigmatism and migraine headaches by visualization.[78]

Even problems in the area of marriage and family life can be helped, according to Silva. A couple can sit facing each other and visualize moments of earlier intimacy and happiness at the Alpha level. This should help to restore marriage harmony.

A more controversial area is Silva Mind Control's claim to develop each student's innate psychic ability. Psychic or invisible spiritual counselors can be visualized who will help with problems. Illnesses can be diagnosed. People who are not present can be visualized and described. Special emphasis is placed on psychic healing.[79]

ORGANIZATION AND GROWTH OF SILVA MIND CONTROL

The world headquarters of SMC is located in the small Texas city of Laredo. The Institute of Psychoorientology, Inc. is the parent organization and does a multimillion dollar business annually. The basic course is taught by Silva Mind Control International in twenty-nine nations. Silva Sensor Systems makes tapes, study aids, and research equipment available to graduates, and manages the Mind Control bookstore. Newsletters for graduates, graduate courses, seminars, workshops, and conventions help promote the Mind Control programs. Mind control research is done by a separate corporation. Special seminars are tailored for executives.[80]

More than five hundred thousand graduates of SMC are reported. Silva Mind Control Centers are found in all fifty states and twenty-nine foreign nations. Each person pays approximately two hundred dollars for a forty-eight-hour course. If a person is not satisfied, money is refunded.

THE ATTRACTION OF SILVA MIND CONTROL

SMC is gaining momentum on college campuses and in academic circles as well as among more prosaic groups. It is being utilized in medical research programs as a coping tool and as an attitude conditioner. The course is free to ministers, rabbis, and priests, and many of these leaders are taking advantage of the offer. Athletes (including the entire White Sox baseball team), political figures, clerks, and truck drivers are involved.

Richard Bach, author of *Jonathan Livingston Seagull*, attributes much of his success to Mind Control. Like Bach, most of the followers say that they were attracted to SMC because it works.

Although costly, SMC is far less expensive than psychoanalysis. The presentations are clear and intensely practical. Unlike est there is little spartan rigidity related to the course.[81]

SECULAR EVALUATIONS OF SILVA MIND CONTROL

Compared with other N.C. groups, SMC has had fewer criticisms. The sales approach is rather low key. Silva's business methods and operations are open to scrutiny. Few doubt the integrity and sincerity of José Silva.

Already we have noted that graduates come from many fields of activity. Most of the graduates are positive in their evaluation. SMC publications cite many examples of how the program is helpful to drug addicts, alcoholics, and the poverty-stricken.

Silva Mind Control publications reflect the fact, however, that there is criticism abroad. There are constant references to criticisms and attempts made to answer them. From the beginning, critics have accused SMC of using a camouflaged hypnotism. Silva and his associates contend that Silva abandoned hypnosis for controlled meditation many years ago. SMC house publications report psychological and psychiatric studies made under Silva Mind Control's auspices. These studies have been made by trained psychologists and psychiatrists. They attempt to establish that Silva Mind Control is safe, beneficial, and useful from a psychological perspective.[82]

Is it hypnotism? Among prominent Silva Mind Control critics are Dr. and Mrs. Elmer Green, biofeedback researchers at the Menninger Foundation in Topeka, Kansas. Since SMC teachers do not use biofeedback machines, Green suggests that there is no proof that students are actually on the Alpha level. For the Greens, Silva's procedure of countdown to the Alpha level is a classic hypnotic technique. The Greens go so far as to contend that Silva Mind Control's semi-hypnotic procedures invoke states which are similar to a trance condition. In such a condition people are open to "possession by spirits." [83]

Is the demonic involved? We have already noted that Silva teaches that invisible psychic advisors can be called up to tell the student what to do. For the Greens, these psychic advisors may serve as masks for evil spiritual forces. These forces may later attempt to control the student's mental, emotional, and physical behavior. Dr. Green's criticism is similar to that of Dr. Shafica Karagulla, California neuropsychiatrist. Karagulla states that unwise tampering with psychic forces can lead to possession by evil spirits.[84]

Students are told by SMC teachers that if psychic powers are used for ignoble or selfish purposes they will be lost. Psychologists contend, however, that posthypnotic suggestions are notorious for their impermanence. If real psychic powers are developed in a student, it can be assumed that the students will use them as they wish—for good or bad—in the future.[85] Dr. Gina Cerminara affirms that every new development of the mind's powers must be accompanied by new moral character and a new power of the heart. Otherwise the N.C. movement will be harmful to our civilization.[86] Such a need could only be met by a dynamic ethical religion such as personal Christianity.

For the Greens, even semi-hypnotic approaches should be used for *acute* situations only, not utilized for *chronic* or continuous situations. Other safer methods for control of physiological and psychological states are available. Hypnosis as a technique has been understood in both the East and the West by spiritual teachers. In the twentieth century, people are in a hurry and desire immediate results with little effort. Hypnotic programming, like LSD, has convinced many people of the reality of the inner dimensions. Because of its power and possible negative effect, however, even semi-hypnotic programs should be confined to closely guarded conditions.[87] The use of hypnotic conditioning by groups such as the Manson Family shows the possible negative use.

Dangers in psychic healing. Other criticisms of SMC include its misleading use of scientific terms and exaggerated claims for powers that can be obtained by anyone who pays the price and takes the course. It is also pointed out that certain powers are not appropriate to certain persons. A notable example is the attempt to diagnose and treat diseases. Dr. Karagulla states that psychic healing has dangers. Some healers can overcharge a person with energy. Large enrollments in classes prevent close contact between teacher and students. If problems arise, they are unlikely to be handled properly even if the teacher has the necessary skill.[88]

Each person is different in the rate by which he can penetrate his unconscious and still keep his feet on the ground. For some, rapid psychic unfolding could lead to destructive neuroses and psychoses. Furthermore, mass programs have difficulty in finding appropriate teachers. As a student progresses, it is important that he have a properly qualified human advisor with whom to talk. In the delicate areas dealt with in Silva Mind Control, the Greens suggest that access to programs should be established on a nonprofit basis. Scientists, such as the Greens, contend that if more responsible control is not established in mind programming, government agencies will have to step in and provide regulation in the interest of public welfare.[89]

THEOLOGICAL EVALUATION OF SILVA MIND CONTROL

It is difficult to classify José Silva from a religious perspective. Coming from a Mexican-American background, he has strong roots in Roman Catholicism. Silva says that he believes in God. He claims that there is nothing in Silva Mind Control that conflicts with Christianity or any other religion.[90]

Close study of the writings of Silva and his associates reveal a view of religion that is far short of the teachings of classical Christianity. Silva defines *reality* as the one dream we all share. We have only the faintest hints of what reality actually is, says Silva. Everything is energy. There is nothing that is not energy. This means that thoughts can influence things and events since they are essentially the same. Even time is energy. Time projects itself ahead with a kind of energy which we can tune in to. When we are in Alpha and Theta levels, we can look into the future as well as the past.[91]

According to Silva, there is a god but he is not interested in man's day-to-day life. The routine affairs are related to higher intelligence. In certain dire emergencies when one needs overall advice of transcending importance, man can turn to God.[92]

Silva teaches that man can communicate with all levels from matter to higher intelligence through Mind Control techniques. These techniques are scientifically provable. Anything beyond this, such as communication with God, is speculation and faith.[93]

These views of Silva border on a view called *Deism*. Deism teaches that God put the universe in motion according to certain laws and God is no longer personally concerned. Other of Silva's views border on pantheism. For pantheism, god and the universe are practically identical.

Practically none of the N.C. groups see God as a personal Father, Lord, or Friend. The image is more likely to be of god as "my ground of being, my true nature, or the ultimate energy." The most common N.C. image of god is the notion of cosmic energy as life force in which we all partake.[94]

Harry McKnight is the director of the Instructor Training Program for SMC. His writings reflect the official view of Silva Mind Control. For McKnight, man is called to be master. Man is fundamentally good. Muslims, Christians, Jews, and Hindus are similar in that they call the same one "our Father" because the father is within us. You can reach Christ-awareness, illumination, and enlightenment for yourself through the Silva method. Doing it yourself is the only way.[95]

In contrast to the SMC perspective, evangelical Christianity sees man as fallen, basically egocentric, and in rebellion against God. The only hope for man's restoration, salvation, harmony, and fulfillment is through the life, death, and resurrection of Jesus Christ. It is obvious that Silva Mind Control is quite different from classical Christianity in its view of man and the remedy needed for man's condition.

4

Erhard Seminar Training (est)

I was told that a man named Werner Erhard had developed the ultimate in N.C. insights in *est*. (spelled with a small "e") The master himself was to be in Houston, and I was invited to his guest seminar.

Before I could reach the top of the steps leading to the meeting site in the hotel ballroom, I was greeted by attractive, smiling est volunteers. As soon as I had paid the admission fee, I was given a large name tag with my first name only printed in large letters. I was greeted as if I were among life-long friends. In a few minutes I found my seat along with several hundred other people in the large ballroom. Next to me on one side was a rather lonely-looking minister's daughter; on the other side I visited with a "seeking" Jewish businessman.

Erhard's assistants came out to tell us what est could do for us. Est would expand our experience of aliveness. Aliveness for est is love, health, happiness, and full self-expression. Est will teach you that you are all right just as you are. If you are not all right, then you will learn that it's all right to be not all right. All of this can be experienced, the bubbly assistant said, in sixty hours for a cost of only $250.

As in the programming of a rock concert, where all builds to the appearance of the star, the evening climaxed with the appearance of Werner Erhard himself. Dressed in formal informal clothing, Erhard breathed self-confidence. With tight slacks and open collar he reflected the California casual look. Sitting on a director-type stool with microphone in hand, he quickly took charge of his audience. "This whole movement called est may be just a big joke," he said. "I could well be a con man and you are being conned. But you will enjoy being conned."

Even in the guest seminar, vituperative language was used. We were told that we all were a bunch of turkeys, tubes, fools, and worse. Words used in relation to sexual intercourse were freely tossed about. In the full training course, shock language seems to be an important part of the technique used. For over an hour Erhard shocked us, ridiculed us, and told us why est is what we needed.

Est, founded by Erhard, has two meanings. It is the Latin word for "it is." Est is also an acronym whose initials stand for Erhard Seminar

Training. The acronym *est* is always written in the more modest lower-case or small letters.[96]

Werner Erhard was born in 1935 in Philadelphia as John Paul Rosenberg. His Jewish father was converted to his mother's Episcopal faith. Little John was baptized into the Episcopal Church. After high school, John Paul held a quick succession of jobs including such work as meat packing, construction, and car sales. Shortly after high school he married his girlfriend Pat, and they had four children.

In 1959, when he was twenty-four, he left his family to escape responsibility. He took off with Ellen, later to become his second wife. There were three children born to this marriage. En route to Saint Louis, John Paul Rosenberg changed his name to Werner Erhard.[97]

The next few years found Werner in California and Washington state engaged in sales work for vacuum business firms and studying N.C. techniques. During this time he picked up many of the ideas he would later incorporate into est. He tried many of the N.C. techniques on the salesmen he trained. He called himself a discipline freak. He either studied or was "into" practically all consciousness groups available in the 1960s.[98]

Werner claims that his business experience has had much to do with what he has learned. Unlike a school or church, he states, a business doesn't care what you do as long as it isn't illegal and produces results. He asked if he could use Zen Buddhism on a sales force. The boss said, "That is great as long as you don't get any on the walls." [99]

One day as Erhard was driving across the Golden Gate Bridge, he states that he saw in a flash of insight what was right and wrong with his life and the N.C. He realized that his life wasn't working and that he was the cause of his problems. Later he summarized his insight by stating, "What is, is, and what was, was, and what isn't, isn't." This experience was the beginning of est. Est means "it is." [100]

Werner put together a new program drawing on varied N.C techniques and materials. Within a month of his so-called Golden Gate experience, he started his est courses. It was as if he had thrown all the pieces of his study and experience up in the air and picked them up as the Erhard Seminar Training.

At first Erhard begged people to take the training. Now he has reversed his pitch and tells people that they don't need training. This reverse psychology has worked.[101]

From a humble beginning, Erhard has developed one of the nation's most talked about and taken N.C. programs. He himself lives like a king, working, and living in two palatial houses, flying leased planes, and driving a Mercedes. Werner claims to sum it all up on his license plate: "So WUT."

Beneath the casual approach reflected in his license plate motto, Werner still studies, observes, and adds on. He has even gone to India to visit and talk with Hindu gurus. Asked what they told him, Erhard reported, "They just told me what is." [102]

THE TEACHINGS OF EST

Erhard and est graduates insist that est can only be experienced, not explained. Werner says that the training seeks to help each trainee to get the sudden enlightenment Erhard himself got on the Golden Gate Bridge. And yet, during the sixty-hour training course explanation accompanies induced experience.[103]

Erhard himself is by temperament a would-be philosopher and a conceptualist. One university professor calls the est seminar "a crash course in epistemology (the doctrine of knowledge)." Others say est has resemblance to the ideas found in the world famous Ludwig Wittgenstein's *Philosophical Investigations.* The est program is grounded in philosophical assumptions about reality and man's relationship to the world.[104] It will be helpful to outline some of Erhard's key teachings and ideas.

A. A basic teaching of est is that the world has no meaning or purpose. This idea is similar to that which we have seen in Zen Buddhism. "What is, is" and "What isn't, isn't" are Werner's summaries.

Erhard states that there are only two things in the world, semantics (words) and nothing. Nothing represents the ultimate truth. Semantics is the form of everything and so represents all that *appears* to exist.[105]

B. A second teaching of est suggests that the mind imposes artificial meanings and purposes on the world. The mind then deceives us into reacting as if reality conforms to these self-imposed "belief systems." We operate on the idea that what we believe is actually so. But this idea is not experiential—it only symbolizes our experience. The mind works with symbols, not direct experience.[106]

Benjamin Whorf, the famous semanticist, states that you have been tricked by your language into a certain way of perceiving reality. We often discard what we perceive that doesn't fit our language structure. Whorf further suggests that an awareness of the mind's trickery can give you insight. Erhard's teachings are quite similar to the concepts of Whorf on this point.[107]

The est program seeks to teach that every system of meaning imposed by outside sources, such as parents, school and church, is illusory.

As we shall see, the major part of the exercises (called processes) in the est training seminar seek to dislodge trainees from their belief systems. In an attempt to destroy belief systems the famous (or infamous) attack or bully approach is used. The cocky trainer bullies his audience into shedding their ego defenses. Abusive language, hours without food or toilet privileges, physical exhaustion, and verbal attacks on the ego are a few of the techniques used.

People are taught to disidentify from their bodies, emotions, and problems. The trainer punctures your ego justifications. You are not allowed to set up systems of behavior that keep you from being still long enough to see your life as it is. You are not allowed to smoke, knit, read, make idle conversation, go to the bathroom, or eat for long periods. You must sit in straight-backed chairs for seventeen hours at a stretch. During the training period you must forego tranquilizers, booze, grass, ups, downs, and aspirins. There are no TVs, watches, or telephones allowed.[108]

When the noise of life has been stopped long enough, you can experience truth, according to est teaching. The truth is: You are. The training allows you to know it with your total being—experientially. This is natural knowing. It is beyond believing, thinking, feeling, sensing, or doing. An enlightened person is one who has learned how to experience the world directly in all its random "suchness." Only what is experienced personally and directly can be true and satisfying.[109]

C. The next step in the teaching program is the emphasis on the fact that as an individual you are the cause of your own world.

Although the true reality is our own experience, we still must function in ordinary reality. This involves accepting life exactly as we experience it to be and then acknowledging that we are responsible for the way we experience it. Life works when you choose what you've got.

Once we choose our experience (what we've got), then it becomes impossible to blame others for our experience. It is resistance to what *is* that causes anguish.[110]

If we blame others for a situation, we attribute *cause* to that other person or situation. We then become the *effect* of that person or situation. We have lost control of our own life. But we are responsible for "sourcing" our own life. As a source, each one of us is god in his own universe.[111]

For years, much of our liberal society has told people that whatever is isn't their fault. Their parents were bad or indifferent or overloving. The president (whoever he is) is a bum. And now est says that people created their own experiences and are responsible for themselves. No wonder est hits like a bombshell for many people.[112]

As a result of the attacks in the training seminar, many people cry, faint, and develop backaches and headaches. In a sudden switch, the trainees are shown how they can make these backaches and headaches dissolve through various exercises in visualization and self-hypnosis. Once you realize that consciousness can alter body states, you are prepared to see that you cause your own world. A corollary is that you can learn to gain control over your own world.[113]

D. The final dramatic step in est is to show the trainee how he can become the author of his own subjective universe of emotions, sensations, and ideas. This is called *getting it*. When you get it you understand that, others can no longer control you. If everything is illusion, then you are free to choose your illusion. You, therefore, control your world. You are free to transform experience through the prism of your own consciousness. Freedom lies in choosing your illusion. You are god in your own universe.

You can create and recreate your *own* experience. This expands your satisfaction. It is *your* mind that has kept you from acceptance and aliveness. It is your mind that has kept you stuck in your own point of view.

When you discover who you are, you also discover that who you are is the source of your ability to communicate. You can re-create your experience and share it with other people. A realistic shared experience, you will find, is of interest to other people because it applies to their own experience.[114]

In order to have this experience or to get it est trainees are shown how to create an inner space. *Inner space* is that space into which a person can retreat and immerse himself in his own consciousness. Once you are in your space, you are taught to construct a little mental room in which you are safe to practice your perfection. The trainer will tell you to pretend you are hammering and sawing and building your space. In your center you mentally place a chair and desk. You are told to build a platform twenty feet above the horizon where you can watch yourself practice your perfection. All this is fantasy. It is to teach you to experience life. Critics ask if this is not a retreat into illusion.[115]

In the seminar, trainees agree not to interact with each other so that they can create their own experience. The seminars are structured so the trainee gets to reexperience his experience. At the same time, the trainee is forced to look at the language and concepts that he is using to describe that experience. He comes to see the difference between the experience and the words and concepts used to describe it.

E. Another est teaching emphasizes that other people should be granted space to create their own experiences. Furthermore, if you want to communicate truly with other people, you must re-create within yourself the other person's intentions. You must learn to flow with another person's experiences. For Erhard love is never having to tell someone else he is wrong. As we shall see, this teaching is a basis for criticism of est.[116]

A relationship with another person is different from an entanglement or involvement. A relationship is being aware of and understanding another person's way of being. To entangle or to involve means to require, to make busy, or to occupy.

THE METHODS AND TECHNIQUES OF EST

One of the secrets of est, for good or bad, is the unique training seminar. We have already mentioned the bully approach. The seminars are psychotheater. The trainers have poise and stage presence. There are moments of catharsis, exhilaration, and then illumination. The seminar uses acting exercises, fantasy, and reverse psychology. I well remember Erhard stating that he and his trainers were really con artists.

In the seminars no note taking is allowed and no written study material is provided. There is no formal discipline to follow and no system to use—it is an experience. You are to get it.

A striking feature of the seminar is the trainer coming on like a marine sergeant with a list of agreements that you *must* make on your own. You are not to talk, wear a watch, take notes, chew gum, knit, read, or sit by someone you know. The bathroom breaks are at least four hours apart and there is one meal per seventeen-hour day. Trainees are reminded that they are more than tubes. The language of the trainer is much like that of a Marine sergeant. He summarizes the "agreement" by saying, "Keep your derriere [he uses a more earthy word] in the room, your shoe soles on the floor, follow instructions, and take what you get." [117]

Not all is negative. In the last hours of the seminar there are words of acceptance and acknowledgement.

THE SOURCES OF EST

As we have already indicated, est is the result of Erhard's experiences with a great host of N.C. techniques. He claims, however, that it was his experience on the Golden Gate Bridge that gave him the critical insight which was the key to the distinctive approach of est.

It should be helpful to note some of the chief background sources of est. Since we have already discussed some of these techniques and groups, a brief reference will suffice.

Careful students will recognize Erhard's heavy dependence on Zen Buddhism and its teaching of no soul and the idea that this world is maya or illusion. Werner comments frequently that Zen is the essential element in est.

Observable is the influence of Mind Dynamics. Mind Dynamics is largely an adaptation of ideas from Scientology and Silva Mind Control. Erhard was an instructor with Mind Dynamics until 1971. Hypnotic induction techniques and visualization were an important part of Mind Dynamics. The est psychic workshop idea comes almost directly from Mind Dynamics. Erhard's use of attack therapy was evidently drawn from the Leadership Dynamics Institute.[118]

Werner was so impressed with Psychosynthesis that he went to Italy to visit its founder, Roberto Assagioli. This system uses techniques of imagery to release the person from the boundaries of words.[119]

Among Western psychologists, Werner has been most influenced by the self-actualization theory of Abraham Maslow and the gestalt therapy of Fritz Perls.

THE ORGANIZATION AND GROWTH OF EST

The est headquarters in San Francisco buzzes like one of America's great growth companies. More than one hundred thousand people have paid $250 to take the training. Waiting lists for training are booked up for months in advance.[120]

Est has a paid staff of more than 250 with some 7,000 inpaid volunteers. The chief executive officer is Don Cox, former teacher at Harvard Business School and General Manager of the Coca-Cola Bottling Company. Est now grosses 10 million dollars or more a year as an "educational corporation." [121]

Est is operated by a trust which claims to run it for the public. Beyond expenses and generous fringe benefits for Erhard and other key employees, est carries considerable philanthropic work. The Werner Erhard Foundation is supported by est. This foundation makes grants for a wide range of consciousness research. The advisory board of est is chaired by a former medical school president. Other members of the board include prominent physicians, scientists, editors, and educators.

The growth of est is primarily promoted by the enthusiastic recommendation of graduates who bring people to guest seminars. The type of people who take est are oftentimes successful leaders who have their material needs met. Most trainees are middle-class whites. Many prominent entertainment people, such as John Denver, Yoko Ono, Polly Bergen, and Joanne Woodward, are est alumni.[122]

Erhard, whose formal education was limited to high school, is proud of the fact that 14 percent of the est graduates are educators. It is curious that the est seminars are filled with verbal people who are enthusiastic about a course that tells them that words and thinking are barriers and so much "bull." [123]

One handicap to the growth of est is the difficulty in finding and preparing trainers. These sub-gurus are in a special category in the organization. Only fourteen have been approved. They are rigorously trained over a long period of time. Few trainers can meet Werner's standards. They are seen not just as teachers but as catalysts who allow experience. The work is hard—eighteen to twenty hours at a time. Perhaps the trainers could not stay in this work if they did not have some vision of helping people.[124]

Despite the difficulty in developing acceptable trainers, Erhard talks about having forty million graduates in the United States alone. Rumors continue to float that he might run for president of the United States some day. Est workshops are projected for Europe. All of these developments are just a few years after est started in a small office above a restaurant in the girlie show section of San Francisco.[125]

Evidently the demand for what est provides is phenomenal. Est could easily get bogged down in organization and in its forms. In the evaluation section, we will think of the impact for good or bad that all of this can have on the future of the United States and the world.

SECULAR EVALUATIONS OF EST

Positive secular evaluations. It is not difficult to find positive appreciation of est. Graduates by the thousands will tell of help received. One psychiatrist reports that after spending fifteen thousand dollars in psychoanalysis she found significant help in this simple, quick, and relatively inexpensive program. She now sends patients to est, claiming that it speeds up the therapy process.[126]

Adelaide Bry, a psychiatrist, has collected positive testimonies concerning the value of est from a number of her medical colleagues. Some like the idea of est, but dislike the form in which it is presented.[127]

Mixed secular evaluations. One well-known New York psychiatrist sees value in the est emphasis on self-responsibility. He feels, however, that est claims to accomplish too much and that its depth is limited. The est emphasis makes change and growth seem too easy.[128]

Negative secular evaluations. Most criticism of est can be classified under five heads.

113

A. Some think est is too authoritarian. A former trainer states that all workers must re-create Werner. For the trainer, est is spiritual fascism. The trainers are not allowed to have any desires or intentions of their own. A true follower of est tends to be a true believer in the negative sense of this phrase. Another former trainer says that Erhard controls information and denies access to it by the media except by official direction. Workers have few rights and privileges. Some suggest that Erhard is losing touch with power as the organization gets larger. This raises the problem of the abuse of power by lesser executives.[129]

B. As was mentioned in relation to Silva Mind Control, some see a similar brainwashing danger in the practices of est. Est devotees contend, in answer to the charge, that the program does not force or cause anyone to believe anything.[130] This statement in turn raises the question as to whether any person can live in a vacuum of formless experience such as that taught by est. There must be some form or belief structure utilized to keep on living. In reality est graduates are taught in a subtle way a world view. Some semi-hypnotic techniques are used to inculcate that view.

C. A third criticism relates to the superficiality of a two-weekend approach to new consciousness. One psychologist states that the est claim to quick enlightenment leads to simplistic beliefs and inadequate understanding. Enlightenment is a life-long process and not a sixty-hour event.[131]

Est advocates insist that the program does not claim to provide enlightenment. Rather est proposes to change a person's ability to experience living. Est is a new approach to knowledge and constitutes only a beginning.[132]

D. A fourth criticism suggests that est creates in followers a stoic resignation to what is. It tends to constitute a retreat from the worlds of history and morality. Est tells about a transformation without moral cost or consequences.

Est followers suggest that graduates are taught to take responsibility for all social contracts. Est, they say, emphasizes responsibility for self and society.[133] Teaching that there is no cosmic frame of reference outside of self, it is difficult to see how est can deliver its followers out of egocentricity into social concern.

E. A study reported in the *American Journal of Psychiatry* warns that there may be a connection between est's authoritarian, confrontational, and ridiculing indoctrinations and psychoses developed by recent trainees. This indoctrination style is also seen as harmful to trainees with weak identities. Some ego defenses are needed as coping mechanisms.[134]

Erhard has replied to such criticims by quoting from independent studies of est graduates. These studies, Erhard states, reveal that incidences of psychoses among est followers is lower than that of the general population. According to Erhard est is not for or against defenses. It gives graduates a choice of which ego defenses they want to use.[135]

We have seen that est attempts to tear down all belief systems. It is difficult to understand how the formless experience advocated by est constitutes a constructive replacement for torn-down belief systems.

THEOLOGICAL EVALUATIONS OF EST

Positive theological evaluations. In her sympathetic book on est, Adelaide Bry cites statements of a number of est graduates who have found est helpful in their religious or theological understanding. A Roman Catholic priest affirms that est gave him the *experience* of what theology had *taught* him. The doctrine of salvation by grace through faith, not of works, came alive, the priest said, after his est training.[136] A young woman minister reported that during her est training, for the first time in her life, she knew God not from faith but directly.[137]

Erhard contends that belief in God is the greatest single barrier to the *experience* of God. When you *think* you have experienced God, you haven't. Experiencing God, for Erhard, is experiencing God, and that is true religion.[138] Erhard further states that his understanding of religion is that it is to provide the space in which experience with God can take place. Est, Erhard says, seeks to support people who create that space and communicate that experience.[139]

The evangelical Christian insists with Erhard that intellectual belief in God and Jesus Christ is not enough. Personal experience is needed. The evangelical skeptic would ask immediately, however, about the nature of God and the avenue which fallen man is to take to find an authentic experience. Est generalities are not sufficient.

One contemporary religious writer has gone so far as to suggest that life changed through est is a "secular salvation." Although the doctrines differ, for John Clark the dynamics of mind transformation are much the same for est as for the revival conversion experience.[140]

The est trainer convinces you that your life doesn't work and then offers you transformation. After you get it, you are urged to take further seminars and to witness for est.

The revival preacher leads you to conviction of sin, and then offers you salvation through Jesus Christ. After conversion, you are urged to attend worship, study doctrine, and witness.[141]

Negative theological evaluations.

A. As we have seen, est teaches that experience has no form to it; it is pure substance without form. The est training is planned to search out and destroy all self-concepts in order to relocate the notion of self in the experience beyond conceptual description. This is getting it. What one gets is that there is nothing to get. All perceptions of reality are illusion. In this experience the trainee is led to see that the entirety of his life, including his self-concept, identity, and conceptual processes, are superfluous to the pure essence of who he really is.

When a person reaches this pure experience state, he is unable to have a critical or evaluative thought. There is no objective reality. If everything is illusion, you are free to choose your illusion. You control your world.

An authentic critical evaluation requires a standard or person external to oneself against which to make an evaluation. Critical evaluation also requires a conceptual thought process by which to judge one idea against another. In est, both the external standard and the conceptual process are seen as barriers to true existence and experience—they are to be eliminated.[142]

For an evangelical Christian, the est viewpoint is not only opposed to the Christian faith and practice but dangerous. Living one's life in terms of a formless experience absolutizes experience for its own sake. It also tends to absolutize whatever social or political situation one is a part of or agreeable with. If experience is not related to value, then injustice is seen as little different from justice. Such an approach could lead to moral and spiritual gullibility and naiveté. The formless existence of est cannot live in a void. The argument of est that value judgments are merely subjective undermines any constructive theological or philosophical discussion of ethics.[143]

The Christian faith teaches a valued universe. The universe was created by a personal God, who initially proclaimed the universe to be good. Even after the rebellion of man, God provided a redemptive plan by which man could find restoration, forgiveness, and harmony with God and others. The est follower is taught to devalue the universe in contrast to the Christian guidelines. A trainee must see himself as perfect as he is. Guilt is an illusion. The need for the cross, resurrection, and second coming of Christ is thus eliminated.[144]

B. In his Golden Gate Bridge experience, Erhard states that he saw that he was going to be no good forever. He realized that he wasn't going to make it or ever be all right. He confronted original sin. But Erhard did not seek or accept God's redemptive grace. He determined to be his own redeemer. He said, "I will say, I am perfect. What is, is all right."[145]

For the Christian there is an eternal difference between right and wrong. All have sinned and come short of God's glory and his purposes for man. We are not perfect. We have lost true happiness and meaning. But despite our sin and imperfection, God has projected a plan which maintains the moral lines of the universe. Jesus Christ, the only perfect one, the God-man, voluntarily died for man's sin. When we turn from the sin that crucified Christ and repent, and accept God's provision for us in Christ, we are forgiven and restored. God loves us in Christ despite our imperfections and sin. By God's grace, as revealed in Christ, we are accepted and seen as perfect in God's eyes. In our lives we seek with God's help to actualize in our daily walk the righteousness imputed to us by Jesus Christ.

C. In the est teaching, the usual N.C. view of God is evident. Erhard states that there isn't anything *but* spirituality. In fact, spirituality is just another name for god, for god is everywhere.[146]

This view is close to the ancient heresy of Pantheism, which identifies god and the world. The Christian theistic view affirms that God created the universe and is immanent in it. God, however, is more than the universe. He is also transcendent in his power and perfection.

PART FIVE
Christian-related New Consciousness Groups
(Adaptations and Distortions)

While living in Cambridge, Massachusetts, I became intrigued with a small seminary which was located in the midst of the Harvard University Campus. It served the church of the New Jerusalem. This church is based on the writings of an eighteenth century Swedish mystic, Emmanuel Swedenborg. His visions gave him an understanding of the Christian religion unlike that of any religious leader before or after his time. In the same Boston area I visited the mother church of Christian Science. Christian Science maintains that the traditional churches have been wrong. The truly spiritual meaning of the Bible and Christianity was revealed to the one who is the promised second coming of Christ—Mary Baker Eddy.

In Washington, D.C., for a visit, I was told I could see the interior of the new Mormon Temple before it was dedicated and closed to non-Mormons. A lecturer at the temple told us that God is supplementing and correcting historic Christianity by materials and revelations given originally to Joseph Smith in the nineteenth century and by continuing revelations to the church president in each generation.

In the twentieth century, a parade of Christian-related groups continues to march into prominence. These groups give lip service, at least, to the classic Christian tradition. Traditional Christian words and doctrines are mentioned. Closer study, however, reveals that many of the teachings of these groups are heretical adaptations or distortions of classical Christianity.

Two representatives of this new breed of Christian-related groups are the Unification Church (Moonies) and the Church of Final Judgment (Process Church).

1
The Unification Church

I first heard of the Unification Church while lecturing and studying in the Far East in the mid-1960s. Visiting in Korea, I was told of the recently completed world tour of a religious leader who considered himself to be the lord of the second advent, or Christ returning as the third Adam. The name of this professed world savior was Sun Myung Moon.

Since 1966, America has literally been inundated with material about Moon and the Unification Church. In fact, Moon moved his world headquarters to the United States in 1973 and announced that the United States was "God's Chosen Land." The United States television and press corps have given us detailed accounts of Moon's activities. Moonies are selling or asking for money in airports and shopping centers. Moon purchased whole-page ads in leading newspapers announcing his support of Nixon during Watergate days. Advertising blitzes tell us that this new church from the East is in the United States to bring more happiness, more hope, and more truth than has been available from any existing religion.

In spite of the reports extolling Moon and the Unification Church, negative reactions are heard from many quarters. I was asked to meet with a group of anguished parents in an Eastern Seaboard state. These parents told of the subtle deceptive manner by which their children were lured into the Unification Church. Once in the church, these parents testified, classic brainwashing techniques were used to capture their children's total personalities. Ex-moonies gave graphic descriptions of the totalitarian way of life which they underwent in the Unification communes.

Who is Moon? What are his teachings? Why has he been able to reach so many intelligent young people? What are Moon's plans for world unification?

The Unification Church is unique in that it is one of the first prominent N.C. groups based on the interpretation of the Christian Bible by a non-Westerner. Orthodox Christian missionaries took the Christian faith and the Bible to Korea some years ago. Now Moon and thousands of Koreans are interpreting the Bible in completely new ways, utilizing

Eastern, new-age concepts. Furthermore, the Moonies are bringing their new religion to the United States where thousands of American young people are embracing it.[1]

Although the Unification Church is not strictly a turn on N.C. group, it is worthy of attention in a N.C. study because of its power and influence. It has shown its ability to completely capture and dominate the lives and imagination of a variety of Americans.

THE ORIGIN AND DEVELOPMENT OF THE UNIFICATION CHURCH

The Unification Church (full name: The Holy Spirit Association for the Unification of World Christianity) was founded by Sun Myung Moon in South Korea in 1954. The story of his life is dramatic and almost unbelievable.

Moon was born in what is now North Korea in 1920. His parents were humble farm folk and members of the Presbyterian Church. In his speech patterns, Moon still reflects his peasant background. Early in his life Moon attended a Pentecostal church. In the 1930s Korean Pentecostals were predicting a new messiah would come from their nation. As we shall see, this idea greatly influenced Moon's thinking. During high school days in Seoul, South Korea, Moon continued his religious interests. In 1936 he went to the mountains to pray on Easter Sunday. During this prayer vigil Jesus appeared to Moon and told him that he was to complete man's salvation, Moon claims. Furthermore, Moon was to be in his own person the second coming of Christ and the new messiah.[2]

After a brief period of study in Japan, Moon returned to Korea. Moon reports that during the period from 1936-1946 God revealed to him the nature of the universe, the meaning of history, and the inner or spiritual meaning of the Bible. Moon also claims to have communicated with Moses, Buddha, and Jesus during this period.[3]

In 1946, Moon relates that he discovered the secret of the world's troubles—Satan had engaged in sexual intercourse with Eve in the Garden of Eden. Moon saw himself as God's chosen representative to reverse the fall of man occasioned by Eve's sin. For an Oriental, a name reveals character or destiny. In keeping with his newly announced destiny, Moon changed his name from Yong (dragon) Myung Moon to Sun Myung Moon. Since Myung means "shining" he is now the shining sun and moon. This title fits his conviction that he is divinity, the beginning and the end, the new messiah. In 1948, the Presbyterian Church of Korea excommunicated Moon for his heretical claims.[4]

North Korea, Moon's home, was captured by the Communists in 1946. Moon claims that he was tortured by the Communists and suffered like

Christ. He reports that he lost consciousness and was thrown out as dead. His disciples carried him away to prepare a Christian burial. Remarkably, he was raised up and in three days was preaching. Moon sees all his life in messianic terms.[5]

Freed by the United Nations forces in 1950, Moon fled to Pusan, South Korea. With the help of a disciple named Hye Won Yoo, he began to formulate and teach his divine principles. By 1954, he had founded the Unification Church in Seoul, Korea. His wife of ten years left him, he claims, because she could not comprehend his mission.[6]

In 1955 Moon was arrested in South Korea on charges of practicing Pikaruna or blood cleansing (a ritual sex ceremony) with the women of his church. The Korean government could not get enough witnesses to testify to prove their case against Moon.

According to Nazarene leaders in Korea, former Unification church members confirm that a teaching of the church in those days required blood cleansing through sexual intercourse with Moon. Since original sin came through Eve's sexual intercourse with Satan, a woman's intercourse three times with Moon (the perfect man) would liquidate her original sin. After the woman's intercourse with Moon, male church members could have sex relations with the perfected women and liquidate their sin. Couples who have experienced this blood cleansing can produce perfect children. Proliferate this blood cleansing widely enough and the world will be saved.[7]

During 1957, the first edition of *The Divine Principle* was published. This book contains the new revelation which Moon claims to have received from God. It is the basis of the Unification Church theology and the key to understanding the Bible.[8]

It was during the mid-1950s that Moon established a close friendship with Colonel Bo Hi Pak. Pak was later to become a high Korean official and help Moon propagate his religion in the United States. In this period, with help from high places, Moon began to develop business interests. Soon he accumulated the great wealth which he was to use for his religious outreach efforts.[9]

Although Unification Church missionaries had been sent to Japan, it was not until 1959 that Moon's doctrines were exported to the United States. Miss Young Oon Kim settled on the West Coast and began translating Moon's writings into English and adapting his program for the American market. She established the first American Unification communes.[10]

As we shall see, it was crucial to Moon's theology for him to find the right wife who would be the perfect mother for mankind and the Holy

Spirit in the Trinity. After three previous marriages (one acknowledged), Moon married an eighteen-year-old high school graduate in 1960 named Hak Jo Han. Moon and Hak Jo Han presently have eight children.[11]

In 1965, Moon visited forty countries spreading his doctrines. During this same period his vigorous anti-Communism campaign brought him the support of South Korea's President Park. In 1969, Moon made a tour of seven major American cities. God led him in 1973, he claims, to transfer world headquarters from Korea to America.[12]

In 1974, Moon led a pro-Nixon rally on the steps of the nation's capital. Similar rallies were held in other American cities. In 1975, Moon announced that he was beginning a program to send missionaries to ninety-five new countries.[13]

THE TEACHINGS OF THE UNIFICATION CHURCH

The Moon teachings constitute a strange religious mixture. Here are some of the ingredients: a. a touch of the Far Eastern flavor of Japan which we have seen in Nicheren Shoshu; b. a trace of the traditional Korean shaman or magician (I saw these shamans and exorcists at work during a visit to Korea); c. occult teachings such as clairvoyance, clairaudience, healing, and spiritualism (Moon claims to have seen visions by the age of twelve. In his presence believers claim to feel spiritual fire and electricity); [14] d. the conviction that the Communists are Satan's chief ally; e. Oriental family worship; f. religion as patriotism; g. remnants from his Presbyterian and Pentecostal roots.

As we shall see, Moon alternates between an extreme literalism and an unfettered allegorizing or spiritualizing in relation to the Bible. For example, Eve's sin is a literal sex act with Satan. On the other hand, the second coming of Christ is dismissed as a premodern myth. The second coming of Christ allegorically means that the lord of the second avent will come in an earthly way from among Christ's followers.[15]

The basic document which contains the teachings of the Unification Church is *The Divine Principle*.[16] This new revelation, divinely revealed to Moon, is needed by mankind to clarify and fulfill the Bible. One is reminded of the importance of the *Book of Mormon* for Latter Day Saints and the dependence of Christian Science on the writings of Mary Baker Eddy.

According to Moon, the universe is founded on certain laws which establish the right relations of things. The most basic law of the universe is the relation between the male and the female. Prior to creating the universe, God existed as internal male subject. God created the universe to provide an external female object. In his relationship with the universe

God was thus fulfilled. This teaching reflects the Chinese Taoist concepts of yin (female) and yang (male), and the place of *Tao* or "the way" in maintaining harmony between the two.[17]

A further expression of duality is seen in the creation of Adam and Eve. As created, Adam and Eve were spiritually immature and were to exist only as brother and sister. God intended for them to have fellowship with him and through this fellowship grow into a spiritual perfection. When Adam and Eve reached this spiritual perfection, they could enter into the relationship of husband and wife. At this point they would form a trinity with God. In addition, Adam and Eve would establish the kingdom of heaven on earth through their perfect children, who would have no inherited sin.[18]

According to Moon, through the centuries Christians have misunderstood the true reason for man's fall and the true way for man's salvation.[19] This informing and saving revelation has now been given to Moon.

Two sexual acts destroy God's plans. Moon explains the fall of man and the way of man's salvation in great detail in *The Divine Principle*. When Adam and Eve were created, Lucifer (Satan) became jealous of God's love for them. Lucifer also saw Eve's beauty and lusted for her. Satan had sexual intercourse with Eve. This sinful act constitutes the *spiritual* fall of both man and Lucifer. Through her sexual union with Satan, Eve took on his sinful characteristics.[20]

Eve soon saw her mistake in consorting sexually with Satan. In an attempt to restore her position with God, she had sexual intercourse with spiritually immature Adam. This sexual act caused the *physical* fall of man. Adam received Satan's sinful characteristics through his sexual union with Satan-tainted Eve.[21]

It is noteworthy that both man's spiritual and physical falls are related to sexuality. Moon has outdone Freud. Through two sexual acts the entire course of human life and destiny has fallen away from God's ideal "Divine Principle." This principle, as we have seen, called for Adam and Eve to slowly grow to spiritual perfection through relations with God. Then they would have been ready to marry and produce perfect children and establish the kingdom of God on earth. But two sexual acts reversed this God-planned relationship.

Cain and communism. The system built up by Moon uses a typological method of interpretation. Moon developed an elaborate typology of two philosophies of life out of the fall of Adam and Eve. As a result of Eve's intercourse with Satan, Cain was born. Cain thus symbolizes man's relationship with Satan. The political expression of this sinful birth is international Communism. Abel is the son of Eve's sex relations with Adam. Abel symbolizes man's relationship with God. Democracy is the political expression of the "Abel-way" of life.[22]

Not only did Moon receive a revelation concerning man's fall but he was also told of the way of man's salvation or the method of reversal of relationships. Through Moon, God was to unfold his plan to restore man to God in both a spiritual *and* physical redemption.

According to Moon, some four hundred years in advance of Christ God sent Malachi to prepare the Jewish nation for the messiah. God also sent Gautama Buddha and Confucius to prepare the Asian world for Jesus. For the Greek or Hellenic world the forerunner for Jesus was Socrates. This meant that it was God's plan for all religions and cultures to unify by accepting Jesus as Messiah.[23]

The unmarried Jesus cannot save us physically. In due time, Jesus came in Adam's place to restore mankind. Although Jesus was not Deity, he was an obedient and a spiritually mature man who was free from original sin. Jesus was to take a bride in Eve's place and produce perfect children and begin the restoration of society and the building of God's kingdom.[24]

Jesus failed in one half of his mission because he was crucified before he was able to get married. Much of the blame is to be placed on John the Baptist, who failed to prepare the mind of the Jews to accept Jesus as the Messiah. When Jesus saw that the Jews would not accept him as Messiah, he decided to at least save men *spiritually* by going to the cross. His crucifixion would pay the indemnity for man's *spiritual* salvation. On the other hand, if he had not been crucified, he could have found a perfect wife and saved man both physically and spiritually. Since he was crucified, another messiah will be needed. For Moon, Jesus Christ did not arise bodily from the grave. He appeared to his disciples only as a spirit being.[25]

Since Christ did not save us physically, no Christian is able to get rid of original sin or remove himself from the lineage of Satan. The lack of physical salvation is the reason for the continued misery in the physical world.

The Bible itself prophesies the date of the coming of a second messiah or the lord of the second advent, according to Moon. The date will be some two thousand years after Jesus (to parallel the fact that Jesus came two thousand years after Abraham).[26]

Moon as the new messiah? The Bible also tells us where the new messiah will be born. The book of Revelation describes "another angel from the east [*rising of the sun*], having the seal of God" (7:2–4, KJV.) Moon teaches that this means that the new messiah will be born in the East. The country of the messiah's birth cannot be Japan because during

World War II Japan was a totalitarian nation which persecuted Korean Christians. It cannot be China, which is a satanic communist state. Korea, on the other hand, is a devout and long-suffering Christian nation. Korea is the place of the new messiah's birth. It is not coincidental that Korea is the land of Moon's birth.[27]

The new messiah will complete the *physical* salvation of man. Since Jesus only accomplished a half-salvation for man, believing in Jesus will only help the spirit man. The new messiah will be greater than Jesus and complete the work of salvation which was only partially accomplished by Christ.[28]

According to the Unification Church teaching, in 1960 the marriage of the lamb which was prophesied in Revelation 19 took place. That is the year that Moon married his present wife. Thus the lord of the second advent and his bride are now becoming the true parents of mankind. The salvation of mankind is on its way.[29]

Unification Church teaching states that in the 1980s the new messiah will be finally revealed to *all* the world. At that time all of the religions of the world will be unified into the Unification Church. Although spiritual debts will have to be paid off by people who have rejected Moon and have evil karma (bad deeds), these debts can be cancelled by work and reincarnations. This means that eventually all men will be saved and the earth will be restored through the unified church and scientific developments which the church encourages.[30]

For proselytizing purposes, the Moon followers do not often make a dogmatic public declaration of Moon as the new messiah. [31] Instead they state that if you come into their meetings and read *The Divine Principle*, you will know that Moon is the lord of the second advent. Ex-Moonies report that once inside the Unification Church they were told that Moon *is* the messiah. In a talk to church leaders in 1973, Moon referred to himself as greater than Jesus or any other religious leader of the past.[32] Statements such as, "I am the Thinker; I am to be your brain" are made. Other declarations made are that "the time is coming when my words will be absolute law" and "I will conquer and subjugate the world." [33]

Despite the Unification Church's ambiguous self-designation as Christian, *The Divine Principle* sees traditional Christianity itself as a hindrance to the work of the new messiah. Christians are like the priests and Pharisees of Jesus' time, the first to persecute the messiah. Because of this opposition Moon states that most Christians are heading for hell.[34]

Following the typology of Cain and Abel and using a signs-of-the-last-days approach, Moon sees the last days before the messiah's public revelation as here. Three events reveal that the old dispensation is ending. Kaiser Wilhelm was the satanic imitation of Adam in World War I. Hitler was the satanic imitation of Jesus in World War II. Finally, international Communism represents the final Antichrist before the end.[35]

In 1960 the new age began. Before the new age can be completed, Communism must be defeated. When the Communists are defeated and Moon accepted as the new messiah, the new spiritual day can open for man. The people who are in the Unification Church are already enjoying new age benefits and in their life are giving the world a preliminary demonstration of this new paradise of total restitution.[36]

THE ORGANIZATION AND GROWTH OF THE UNIFICATION CHURCH

In 1973 the world headquarters of the Unification Church was moved to the United States. The forty-two story former New Yorker Hotel has been transformed into the headquarters building. The former Columbia University Club near Times Square in New York City is also a part of the Moon operation. In fashionable Westchester County near New York City, the Unification Church has purchased three large estates for some 8 million dollars. In upstate New York on the Hudson River, a 258-acre Roman Catholic seminary has been purchased for more than 1.5 million dollars. It is to be used as a Unification Church training center. Around the country the church owns dozens of church-commune centers in major cities and near college campuses. Ranches are maintained for training centers.[37]

The Unification Church claims more than thirty thousand American adherents. It has living centers set up in 120 American cities and recruiting teams covering 150 college campuses. The top Moon aides live in sumptuous style while the masses of Moonies live in abject poverty, huddled in sleeping bags or unheated vans. Moon himself lives in a twenty-five room mansion on a twenty-six-acre estate. Moon justifies his affluent life-style in two ways. In materialistic America, Moon says, we need to show the wealth and strength of the church. Many senators, congressmen, and V.I.P.'s will be impressed. Furthermore, Moon claims, "I am extremely wealthy myself. I don't use money from Moonies for my own person coffers. I don't need it." [38]

Moon claims to have some one thousand churches and 360,000 members in South Korea. Many of the Korean college students and disenchanted intellectuals who join say they want a chance to be a part of Moon's higher purpose. This purpose, they say, seeks to unify all the world's faiths, suppress Communism, and achieve recognition for Korea as the world's new holy land. A significant part of the Unification Church's appeal to the Koreans is related to patriotism.[39]

In Japan there are some forty-thousand Unification Church members with a concentration of membership in the rural areas. Without giving specific details, the Unification Church claims to have 3 million followers in 120 countries around the world.

In the United States church, local decisions are referred to the directors of each of the 120 houses or communes. The ultimate decisions come from the world headquarters. The Moon quest for world unification has a complicated, highly efficient organization. The annual budget for the United States operation alone is reported as more than eleven million dollars.

What are the practical explanations of Moon's financial growth in Korea? Moon's Korean business interests have prospered under the rule of President Park. His business concerns have received government privilege. He has been granted numerous corporate tax exemptions. The church members staff and operate his businesses and take very small stipends or no salaries at all. This means that Moon can undercut the market when necessary to sell his products. Among Moon's interests are such businesses as pharmaceuticals, heavy equipment manufacturing, and titanum and ginseng tea exportation. In 1973 Moon reported that he had thirteen million dollars in his own personal bank account.[40]

What about the sudden political and financial growth of the Unification church in the United States? In 1969 there were less than 250 moonies in the United States. They were dedicated but poor. A number of explanations are given for the political and financial support which Moon received in America in such large measure in the last few years. It is suggested that money came from: a. Moon's prospering Korean businesses which grew with the help of government favors and semi-free labor; b. Right-wing Japanese anti-communist businessmen (some report two million dollars from one Japanese man for Moon's first American crusade); c. the United States government—illegally through secret diplomatic channels; d. the Korean government and the Korean CIA through the Korean Cultural Foundation (Ironically President Park's government in Korea has sent hundreds of Christian leaders to jail in the past few years. Stoner and Parke spell out the evidence that the Unification Church could have been a part of a multimillion dollar campaign supported by Korean leaders. This program of propaganda, influence-buying, spying, and bribery was aimed at assuring the United States's continued support of President Park's regime in South Korea. In any case, the Unification Church influenced American public and legislative opinion in favor of South Korea and its government.); e. the work of the thousands of young people who have joined the Unification Church in the United States.[41]

In addition to seeking to win converts, the Unification Church has a highly organized program to influence people in high places in the United States Federal Government. In one speech Moon envisioned three good-looking female moonies assigned to each senator. A Washington newspaper columnist wrote about one young Moon lady who established a special relationship with the then Speaker of the House, Carl Albert. One Moon plan has government leaders invited to a hotel to have dinner and hear lectures and see films about Moon's work. Moonies work to elect selected congressmen. Campaigns were mounted to support President Nixon. Massive letter-writing campaigns were carried on to influence bills favoring South Korea.[42]

Much of this activity seems wrong for a church which gets a nonprofit exemption. The Internal Revenue Service code specifies that a nonprofit church, such as the Unification Church, shall not use its earnings to carry on propaganda or influence legislation or intervene in the political campaign of candidates for public office.[43]

THE RECRUITING AND LIFE-STYLE OF MOONIES

I have observed Moonies in group prayer. Some cry and others jerk spasmodically as they pray. I noticed a glassy, spaced-out look in their eyes. On their faces is a perennial smile. All devout religious people understand something of what it means to get high on God, but Moonies seem to have an unusual, faraway, slightly-dilated look in their eyes. This look has caused them to be described as moonstruck, moon-washed, or moon-merized.[44]

How do Moonies get this way? What is their background? What is their life-style after they are recruited?

The actual story of a Moonie's recruitment and life in a commune. In recent years I have talked with a number of ex-Moonies. One charming and intelligent ex-Moonie of my acquaintance has described in great detail her recruitment and her life as a Moonie. Her story is an almost exact duplicate of thousands of other middle-class American Moon converts. I will use her personal story as a typical model to describe the recruiting and life-style of the Moonies. In order to protect her and her family I will not use her real name and will omit references to specific places.

Well-educated, attractive, from a wealthy home, Mary had just finished some work in a prominent university graduate school. She went to visit a cousin in a Western city. Searching for a job, she noticed an advertisement in the classified section of a local newspaper. It said simply: "If you're interested in humanitarian work, contact . . . ." and gave a tele-phone number. (In addition to newspaper ads, many are invited to introductory sessions by Moonies who work the campuses, churches, libraries and airports.) Mary called and was invited to a meeting at a former sorority house, near the local university, which had been turned into a Moon center. There she found a group of warm, happy people, most of whom were in their twenties, who seemed to want to help people. (In major cities, the Unification Church has houses which are communal centers for young, single members and meeting places for the whole group.)

Mary was a religious person. She was attracted by the thirty-minute period of singing which included many familiar hymns. She was moved by the testimonies of the attractive members present who told what the movement had meant to them. She was told that the Unification Church would help unify all races and religions. Members of different races were present.

Mary liked what she saw and agreed to attend a weekend workshop. (This is the next step for people who want to be taught the basis of the joy and happiness of the group members.) Everything was positive. Mary said that this was a welcome change since everything had been so nega-tive in college. There was no drinking, smoking, or dirty jokes. The people seemed to care for her.

During the workshop an attractive lecturer told about a book called *The Divine Principle*, which was the basis of the Unification Church teaching. Mary reports that everything seemed to be in this book. It made things clear. The lectures showed how the Unification Church was seeking to meet the practical needs of the world. It gave the answers to the big questions. Mary began to think that whoever wrote the book was a genius. She was ready to hear more.

During the last lecture session of the workshop, reports Mary, she was told that the person who wrote *The Divine Principle* was the new messiah. His name was Sun Myung Moon. Mary said she began to cry after the lecturer talked about how the Jews had persecuted Jesus. The lecturer then said that he didn't want the Christians to make the same mistake and persecute the second messiah.

That night, after the last lecture, Mary could hardly sleep. In a dream she saw a white light coming and going. She heard a voice saying, "Mary, you are to be a mother of creation." The director told Mary the next morning that she was beginning to enter perfection. She was a spiritual child. Mary then decided to stay on and join the Unified Family (another more intimate name for the Unification Church).

After a few days Mary was sent to a seven-day intensive training camp at a rather isolated rural retreat (new recruits are brought to the retreat center at night to help create a sense of disorientation). There were more lectures on *The Divine Principle*. The lectures became more emotional. They were held in the mornings and until eleven in the evenings. She was taught the importance of obeying those above her in the Unified Church. There was no smoking, no drinking, no sex. "All we did was sing and talk about love and our true parent," Mary reports. A long-time member of the group was with Mary constantly. The schedule was disciplined. Sleep was limited. There was little time to relax or talk about casual matters. At the same time there were displays of affection and hugs, hand-holding, and smiles.

By this time Mary was all charged up and ready to go back to the city to work on fund raising. In the meantime, she was told about the Unification Church regulations. She was to make arrangements to transfer all her possessions to the Unification Church. Mary was also told that everyone not in the movement was dominated by Satan and should not be trusted. This warning extended to parents and close friends.

Finally Mary was ready to begin a regular work schedule. It only allowed five or six hours of sleep each day. Instructions were given on how to raise money.

Everyday, Mary reports, she boarded a van and spent at least twelve hours a day peddling flowers and candy on street corners and in businesses. Regardless of weather conditions, the van rolled. Even as a beginner, Mary took in more than one hundred dollars a day. She began to learn about heavenly deception. This means that you can tell any kind of lie to sell. Satan deceives God's children so Moonies are justified in deceiving Satan's children. She was told that the money taken in went to help mankind. She and the other Moonies were fed peanut butter sandwiches and occasionally spaghetti. On some days there were fasts.

When she was not selling, Mary was praying and studying *The Divine Principle*. Mary was told that if she left the Unification Church she would die spiritually and be possessed by Satan physically.

Mary was told that the more she centered her every thought on God the more money she would collect. Mary stated, "I was all built-up. I thought I was working for God in taking the money from Satan's children."

Mary was deprogrammed before she became heavily involved in recruiting and took later steps in the Unification Church program such as marriage. In about three years it is possible for a Moonie to achieve perfection and marry a perfect mate chosen by the movement.

Perfection, however, cannot be reached until you have received Moon's blessing. This requires years of devoted work. In addition, to get the blessing you must recruit and bring three new spiritual children into the church. Then you can be married. Before that you must remain totally celibate.

Unless you are married you do not have complete salvation. To be married you have to win converts. This means that every Moonie is on the streets searching for converts. College students, you are told, are vulnerable during dead week. Watch for the lonely. The backpack and the guitar case are symbols of rootlessness, and those carrying them are prime prospects.[45]

In keeping with the Unification Church teaching already discussed, a husband and wife do not have true marital status until they are spiritually blessed in marriage by the true parent—Moon. God's plan was for Adam and Eve to live as brother and sister until they could mature enough to be married. When you have achieved maturity (after years of work and recruiting), then you can have a true marriage blessed by Moon, and your children will be pure. You are then a part of God's plan to reestablish the kingdom of God on earth.[46]

Marriage is a crucial step in the Unification Church program. It is so important that Moon himself or his appointed representative must apply the divine principle in matching suitable types. If the couple is perfectly matched, then the children will be potentially perfect. This system is obviously influenced by the Oriental custom of arranged marriages. Moon urges international and interracial marriages. According to Moon's plan, all men will one day be unified and clearly defined skin colors and races will disappear.[47]

Moon likes big weddings. Recently in a Seoul, Korea, sports arena, Moon married eighteen hundred couples from twenty-four countries, including seventy couples from the United States.

After marriage, Moonies must live separately for at least forty days, longer for younger and more immature members. Even after this period of enforced celibacy, church couples tend to live as brothers and sisters in the Unified Family. To separate off as couples impairs the cohesiveness of the community.[48]

Children slow down fund raising and so members are discouraged from having children until they are thirty-five. Abortion is condoned by the church.

Every Sunday morning at exactly five o'clock, as a member of the Unification Church you gather with others for a pledge service. A picture of Moon is before you. You bow down three times to the heavenly Father and to the true parent (Moon). Then you recite an elaborate pledge of undying loyalty to the one true parent (Moon). The final phase, "This I pledge and swear," is repeated three times.[49]

Holy salt is carried at all times. This salt is to be used to sanctify all food and all rooms where you stay outside the commune. The holy salt is also used for sickness. Members are urged to learn the Korean language since it will eventually become the one universal language.[50]

An actual case of deprogramming. Now to return to the story of Mary. Because of the distance to Mary's home, she delayed longer than usual the trip home to get her car and her other possessions in order to turn them over to the Unification Church. In Mary's particular case, a wealthy father and an older brother concocted an elaborate plan to free her from the Unification Church when she returned home to get her possessions. Her father forcibly held her while the controversial Ted Patrick, author of *Let Our Children Go!*, deprogrammed her. Her father reports, "We had to force her to stay. If we had not, she would have been gone forever. I was terrified—that she would go insane, commit suicide, or be kidnapped by the deputation of Moonies sent to get her back."

The father further commented, "We knew the Moonies were in town, and we were ready with guns. The neighbors were alerted and kept watch. I got a peace bond (legal restraining order) on the Unification Church leader who was in town to take her back."

One statement by Mary's father reveals something of the plight of parents. "I know this sounds crazy, but I was scared. The Moonie leaders have some kind of occult power. If they got to her, they could make her go back. I couldn't get help from anyone. I tried the police, the F.B.I., the churches. Either they don't believe it or they think that your daughter is some kind of religious kook."

In his desperate plight, the father reports, "The only thing I could do was to kidnap her and force her to sit still and think the whole thing through. I was afraid she was too far gone. She was told that everybody and everything outside the Unification Church was controlled by Satan. They told her that if you don't side with the Church, you will be killed. She was terrified."

Mary gives her side of the story. "I was getting ready to go back to the Unification Church after collecting all of my things. I agreed to go to breakfast at my father's house. When I walked in, there was Ted Patrick at the door. I knew his name because the church had warned us about him. I tried to leave. They forced me to stay. Daddy had barred the windows and changed all the locks on the doors."

Mary has given some of the details of her deprogramming. "Ted Patrick

132

outlined in detail things that go on in the church. He told me about Moon's background. He showed me the materials written about Moon. He read from some literature that I would have to write an autobiography of my sex life before I could be blessed by Moon. That really did it. I don't have to confess anything to anybody but God. And Moon is not God."

The physical change in Mary was noteworthy. She said that when she began to think, her legs and arms became very weak and her pupils shrank. She thought she had been drugged. Mary commented, "My mind had been operating on a different level because of the programming I had had in the Unification Church. The change in coming off that level was what made me feel so strange."

Ted Patrick claims that he has deprogrammed more than a thousand young people from groups like the Unification Church. Patrick maintains that the Unification Church uses the fear of Satan to destroy the free will. They convince you that your mind is evil and is of Satan. Patrick admits that he argues, yells, screams, reads the Bible, and shows the young people negative literature about the group in which they are involved. He claims that he must force the young person to think even if it takes an eighteen- or twenty-hour session. Even after he has broken through, Patrick maintains that an around-the-clock vigil must be kept for a period to prevent contact with cult members.

The Unification Church is aggressive and sought to retain Mary in the church. The leader of the commune and other members where Mary belonged drove several hundred miles to seek to recover her. The leader gave an interview to the local press in Mary's home city. The leader maintained that there is no mind control or hypnotism in the Unification Church. "We are Christians," he said, "nobody is forced to stay with us." "Mary," he said, "was a dedicated member when she went home to get her things. She joined us of her own free will." The Unification leader accused Ted Patrick of kidnapping and forcing Moonies to renounce the church. He further commented, "I would like to meet with Mary. I am curious about what happened. Overnight she became an entirely new person."

Mary has not only renounced the Unification Church but has helped form an organization of ex-Moonies to combat the Unification Church and others like it. She claims that college students especially need to see the danger of a group like the Unification Church. Mary cites her own case: "I had an open mind and was searching for meaning. I was feeling cynical and at a loss for what I could do. I was tired of negativism. Then came Moon with all the answers. I was ready for him." Mary suggests that the Unification Church tried to hold her by separating her from her family

133

and using Bible verses to inculcate fear. "They kept me from thinking, because if I had thought, I would have had doubts."

Already we have indicated some of the reasons why Mary and others like her become involved in the Unification Church. Let us recapitulate and mention other reasons. Mary wanted a sense of constructive purpose. She wanted to build a better world and feel useful. She needed a challenge. Because of her family's inherited and (in her generation) unearned wealth, she had a sense of guilt. She wanted love and a sense of belonging.

Why did Mary succumb to the Moon group so easily and quickly? She suggests that she was wishy-washy in her personal philosophy. She had no deep-seated religious or intellectual convictions. Mary, as indicated above, places some of the blame on her university teachers. They seemed to say, "The church is bad, the crime situation is bad, the capitalistic system is bad. I was ready for a positive approach—with answers."

SECULAR EVALUATION OF THE UNIFICATION CHURCH

Evaluating a movement as complex as the Unification Church is a formidable task. Already, in the course of our descriptions of Moon, we have pointed out a number of the church's problems and weaknesses. Others can be suggested.

The Unification Church practices deception in at least two ways. A. Aware of its poor image in certain areas, the Unification Church uses aliases and names that sound constructive or similar to mainline religious groups. One recruit was lured into the Unification Church through the attraction of a Moon front organization called "One World Crusade." Other front organizations under the Unification umbrella include the International Cultural Foundation, The Creative Community Project, and the Collegiate Association for the Research of Principles. Who would not want to help the International Federation for Victory over Communism, the Freedom Leadership Foundation, and the American Youth for a Just Peace? Scientists are attracted to the International Conference on Unified Science. People interested in the artistic world are reached through the Korean Folk Ballet and the New Hope Singers International. The athletic type are sought through the D.C. Striders' Track Club. Very few of these groups have made public that they are controlled by or affiliated with Moon and the Unification Church.[51]

B. The other type of deception is called heavenly deception. In order to sell their products or win converts, the Moonies are taught that it is appropriate to lie or deceive. The theology of this deception is based on

134

the idea that Satan deceived God's children and so the Moonies are justified in deceiving Satan's children (the general public).[52]

Some contend that this heavenly deception is practiced in areas more significant than selling candy and flowers. Investigation of questionable church activities are now being carried on by the Internal Revenue Service and the United States Naturalization and Immigration Service. We have already noted the church's seeming violation of the law restricting political activities by tax-exempt religious organizations.

Brainwashing and mind control. Many astute critics see a resemblance between what is variously called brainwashing, coercive persuasion, or mind control and the techniques utilized by the Unification Church in the takeover of Mary's personality. Perhaps the best modern example of mind manipulation is the technique developed by the Chinese Communists in the Korean War. Robert J. Lifton in *Thought Reform and the Psychology of Totalism* sees the "religious totalism" used by Moon as similar to the techniques used by the Chinese Communists.[53] We remember that Moon himself was a North Korean Communist prisoner in the late 1940s. Rabbi Maurice Davis points out that the Unification Church uses some techniques similar to those used by the Nazis in Germany.[54]

Ronald Enroth contends that the Unification Church techniques cause young people to accept ideas, attitudes, and behavior completely foreign to them prior to their involvement in the group. Hare Krishna uses many of the same techniques.[55]

Review the experiences of Mary mentioned above in the light of Lifton's listing of the Communist techniques. These techniques are sensory deprivation (food and sleep), imposition of guilt and fear, dramatic change of world view, and stripping of identity.[56]

Mind control and total commitment are further engendered by the Unification Church with the aid of conditioning techniques. R. M. Kanter describes these techniques. They include a call to total sacrifice, investment of all tangible resources in the group, giving up of personal privacy and even two-person relationships for group devotion, separating children from parents for rearing or schooling, and the magnifying of new converts' strong points. Other techniques suggested are: stressing the exclusivity of the group's belief system and path to salvation; insisting on constant group meetings and group rituals; the magnification of persecution; and the magnifying of a charismatic, authoritarian leader.[57]

The wrong kind of commitment. It is obvious that the Unification Church, perhaps more than any New Consciousness group, other than Hare Krishna, utilizes the above-mentioned mind-control techniques. A major problem facing young people, parents, the courts, the schools, and the churches in the United States is how to differentiate between a constructive commitment and a destructive one. Commitment and conversion are at the heart of authentic religion. Commitment is a part of legitimate patriotism and a dynamic and meaningful life. On the other hand, when commitment is unrestrained, indiscriminate, unevaluative, and coerced, it is harmful and destructive.[58] The Unification Church approach is seen by many as unevaluative and coercive—at least after the initial step into the group by the convert has been taken.

THEOLOGICAL EVALUATION OF THE UNIFICATION CHURCH

A recent study commission appointed by the National Council of Churches declared the Unification Church heretical from a Christian perspective. Jewish and Catholic leaders joined the major Protestant groups in denouncing Moon's church as a breeding ground for anti-Christian, anti-Semitic, and anti-democratic beliefs. More conservative Christian groups are likewise critical of the Moon theology. It will be helpful to list some representative Christian criticisms of the teachings of the Unification Church.

A. The Unification Church does not accept the Bible as the normative and inspired standard of Christian doctrine. For Moon, the Bible needs his teaching as found in *The Divine Principle* for clarification and fulfillment. Some parts of the Bible which are accepted are over-literalized and distorted by Moon. Other parts of the Bible such as the teaching about the second coming of Christ are demythologized and dismissed by the Unification Church. In some cases the Bible story is deliberately changed as can be seen in the Moon account of the birth of Cain.

B. The biblical teaching about Jesus Christ is either distorted or ignored. The New Testament sees the cross as an essential part of God's redemptive plan. The Unification Church sees Christ's death on the cross as a second-best and partial redemptive act. Other weaknesses of Moon's theology include his denial of Christ's divinity and physical resurrection. The crucial heresy is related to Moon's identification of himself as the lord of the second advent, replacing the second coming of the risen Christ.[59]

C. The doctrine of the Trinity is distorted by Moon. The Holy Spirit is seen as the true mother or the wife of Moon. Jesus is not seen as divine and coeternal with the heavenly Father.[60]

D. The fall of man is seen by Moon as the result of the sexual sin of Eve with Satan. The idea of the two falls (spiritual and physical) is dualistic and foreign to orthodox Christian belief. From the classic Christian perspective, God limited himself in giving the first man and woman freedom. They used this freedom to rebel against God. The Bible does not relate

136

the fall of man to Eve's sexual sin with Satan.[61]

E. A further heresy relates to the Unification Church's teaching that a Christian must await Moon's advent and ministry to receive complete salvation.

Is not James Bjornstad right in stating that Moon's theology and Christian theology are separate and distinct, and mutually exclusive? [62] From the viewpoint of Christian orthodoxy we could go further in saying that the Unification Church fits the dramatic biblical description of Satan coming to deceive man under the disguise of an "angel of light" (2 Cor. 11:14).[63]

F. The Unification Church corrupts and distorts an authentic, biblical, and ethical perspective. It pays little attention to the moral guidelines of the Old Testament prophets and the restatement and reinterpretation of their message by Jesus. It puts a divine halo around Korea and the United States, good or bad. Moon has had no prophetic word about President Park's persecution of Christians in Korea. During Watergate days the Unification Church declared that God revealed to Moon that he had chosen Nixon to be president of the United States.[64]

For Moon there is no final judgment or hell. Even the evil spirits can work off their indemnity in reincarnations and be saved.

THE CHRISTIAN, MIND CONTROL, DEPROGRAMMING, AND RELIGIOUS FREEDOM

What does Christian theology have to say about the problems of mind control, deprogramming, and religious freedom? These areas are beset with pitfalls. Two statements by the Unification Church reveal that Moon is aware of the fact that America is a fertile religious field and that he intends to use any method available to reap the ripe harvest he sees in America. In 1971 the Unification Church published a pamphlet in which it said, "Since the Church is the safest and most recognized form of social organization, Mr. Moon founded the Unification Church in 1954 to have the greatest freedom of action." [65] In a recent television interview the United States president of the Unification Church said that the Moonies use the most effective techniques they know to recruit and teach members, and that if they could find a better way, they would start using it tomorrow.[66]

Moon realizes that America is unique among the world's great nations in its treasured law on religious freedom. This law protects the right of a United States citizen to believe any religious idea and affiliate with any religious body. This unique idea of religious freedom was not always appreciated even by religious leaders. The famous Puritan leader, Cotton Mather, wrote to a ship commander suggesting that he waylay the ship coming from England carrying William Penn and his heretical Quakers and sell the whole lot as slaves. Mather further told the commander that in so doing he would perform a service to the Lord.[67] Some Christian leaders approximate Mather's attitude toward the Quakers in their opposition to Moon and his followers.

The Unification Church and other cultic groups warn of the dangers inherent in seeking to repress or deprogram unpopular religious groups. Conservative critics of Moon respond by stating that he and other cult leaders have taken advantage of America's "religious liberty concept and used it in a way unforeseen by our Founding Fathers." Civil libertarian groups contend that youths of legal age have a right to practice any religion they choose. Jean Lyles states that parents have had eighteen years to transmit their religious and cultural values to their young. There comes a time when the parent must let go and hope for the best. Young people must be given freedom even if it is the right to make a wrong choice.[68] Berkeley Rice says that if you question the right of youth to join the Moonies you may soon begin to question the right of grown-ups to seek salvation or new consciousness in such socially acceptable adult groups as Transcendental Meditation, Arica, est, and Primal Therapy.[69]

Social critics point out that the media uses subtle mind-control techniques in seeking to induce everyone to consume alcohol, which is a proven depressant and potentially harmful to vast numbers of Americans. Psychologists remind us that evangelical Christians and other acceptable religious groups constantly engage in personal witnessing and evangelism with intensity and zeal. Emotional songs are sung as a skilled minister seeks to lead people to be converted to a new and different way of life.

Cult leaders claim that if they use brainwashing, the deprogramming techniques of men like Ted Patrick are little more than "counter-brainwashing." Cult leaders are quick to give accounts of highly emotional deprogramming sessions of twenty hours or more. Deprogrammers reply that they are simply seeking to break the chain of fear and guilt and force an objective evaluation of unexamined beliefs. The goal is not to force the person to accept a new belief.[70]

Enroth, an evangelical Christian, contends that one has a right to enter a cult group freely. The big question, however, is whether one is capable of exercising any free will after the mind-control program of the cult has been employed on the convert for a period of time. Does not the American Constitution allow freedom of thought, speech, and association as well as freedom of religion? Ex-Moonies testify that they were so programmed by the Unification Church that something like deprogramming was a necessity if they were to be rescued.[71]

Evangelical Christians, in particular, insist that no American legal ruling should be established that would in any way hinder their right to lead people to a self-willed religious conversion. Evangelicals insist, however, that they do not want the right to practice coercive conversion. The person must retain his right to say no at the beginning or even further along his religious pilgrimage.

The Unification Church has announced that it is seeking a better image in America. Tremendous sums of money are being paid to public relations firms to help them in this regard. Would not a step forward for the Unification Church be a policy allowing any member of their group at any time to have open conversation with parents and friends on neutral sites? These conversations should allow the young people to evaluate fully and freely all the dimensions of life in their cultic group.

In any case, parents of Moon converts and the converts of other cultic groups will undoubtedly continue to seek to help and free their children. The courts will continue to struggle with ways to help the parents without resorting to kidnapping. At present the method of temporary legal conservatorship by the parents of the child is being allowed. Civil libertarians insist that this plan is a major defeat for religious liberty in the United States.[72]

Let us remember Mary's testimony concerning the reasons why she went into the Unification Church so easily and quickly. She had few clear-cut religious convictions. She had no real purpose or cause. Her society and university were too negative.

The Spiritual Counterfeits Project is a group which seeks to equip Christians to understand the cults in depth. The group further seeks to enter into the cultic system of belief and expose problems in the cult's own terms. It also seeks to develop broad Christian answers to the needs met by the cults. It points out that deprogramming is not conversion, and people cannot live in a vacuum.

The work of the Spiritual Counterfeits Project clearly implies that there are lessons which Christians can learn from groups like the Unification Church. In *Turning East,* Harvey Cox suggests ways to meet the challenge of the non-Christian cults. Among other ideas, he mentions the need to create churches which are communities of love, where Christian people listen and take individuals seriously. Warm, direct Christian experience needs to be engendered. An emphasis on Christian sacrifice, discipline, and challenge must be recovered. Young people should be given a unified spiritual vision of self, society, and the cosmos. Definite spiritual techniques should be taught and demonstrated. In short, the churches must be seen as places where one can get a broad spiritual vision and where one can find a place for spiritual growth and development.[73]

2
The Process Church of the Final Judgment (Process)

It was a warm and humid day in Houston. Most of us were in shirtsleeves. And yet here were young people in long black robes standing on the street corners. By their sides were huge German Shepherd dogs. I noticed an inverted swastika-like cross symbol on their robes. They were selling magazines emblazoned with intertwined symbols of Satan and Christ. Who are these young people? Why are we interested in them in a study of N.C. groups?

The Process Church of the Final Judgment is the rather ominous name of the group which these young people represent. This church is an extreme example of the nonorthodox and heretical use of Christian and biblical symbols. The group is concerned with altering consciousness, attitudes, and motives. It has been accused of influencing the life and thought of Charles Manson and his "family." Process has a sense of urgency since it predicts that these are the last days of human civilization.

THE ORIGIN AND DEVELOPMENT OF PROCESS

One of the most recent N.C. groups, Process is the brainchild of Robert de Grimston, a London architect. Born in 1935, de Grimston comes from a High Anglican background. In earlier days, de Grimston was an active disciple of Ron Hubbard and a leader in Scientology circles. Anne, his wife, was a spiritualist medium. In the early 1960s de Grimston began an intensive religious search involving dream interpretation and the study of the Bible and other scriptures. Soon he gathered a group of followers. By 1970 his followers called him the "Recorder" or "Oracle," He allowed his hair to grow in a way that made him look like the traditional picture of Christ. Some of his followers even thought of him as a reincarnation of Christ.[74]

The movement shifted into a formalized religious body under the formidable name of The Process Church of the Final Judgment. The members give up their family name such as Smith and Brown and became Brother Micah or Joab or Sister Rebekah. The London headquarters building was luxurious. It was reported that a number of well-to-do Englishmen left extensive legacies to the movement.[75]

In the mid-1960s, de Grimston and his followers reported that they were directed by the spirits to go to Mexico. There they settled in the Yucatan peninsula at a Mayan ruin, Xtul. In Mexico they claim to have received a series of religious revelations from discarnate entities.

In the late 1960s Process launched extensive recruiting drives in the United States. Vincent Bugliosi, district attorney in the Manson trial and author of *Helter Skelter,* claims that the Process members were in Los Angeles and San Francisco at the time when Manson was organizing his family. In fact, headquarters for the Process group in San Francisco was only two blocks from the place where the Manson Family lived in Haight-Ashbury. My first knowledge of both the Process group and the Manson Family was gained during my visits to Haight-Ashbury in the late 1960s. Bugliosi believes that Manson was influenced by Process thought at this time. The Process leaders deny direct contact with Manson and his group.[76]

In the 1970s the Process group moved their headquarters and chief operations to the United States. A number of young people from wealthy English families came with them, including the daughter of an English lord.[77]

THE TEACHINGS OF THE PROCESS CHURCH OF THE FINAL JUDGMENT

The Process doctrine is an original combination of historic Christian symbols and Eastern religious and philosophical ideas. God is manifested or refracted through four gods or symbols: Jehovah, Lucifer, Satan, and Christ. All of these gods exist in all of us in varying mixtures. Jehovah is that part of us that is vengeful and calls for courage and ruthlessness. Lucifer is that part of us that urges us to a life of enjoyment, artistic sensibility, and harmony (Lucifer is not to be confused with the fallen angel of the Bible). Satan stands for that part of us that is divisive, lustful, corrupt, and depraved. Christ stands for reconciling love. The Jehovah, Lucifer, and Satan "powers" within us are engaged in a cosmic game of antagonism (this idea was taken from Scientology). This game is a process of hate and blame.[78]

Why men should love Satan. The Christ-power within us comes to the rescue. It works to reconcile the three different gods or powers, Jehovah, Lucifer, and Satan, which are in conflict within us. The Christ-power, as an underlying positive deity within us, enters and reveals that blame is our problem. Christ teaches that we are to love that which we would normally hate. Christ refused to hate Satan. This love stopped the old game of hate and blame and initiated a new game or *process.* Jesus cast aside all tendencies to feel guilt for sin or to blame others. Since Christ loves Satan, Processeans love Satan and are devoted to Satan.[79]

The Process teaching is applied to many areas of life. In sexuality, for example, our teachers, parents, and churches are conditioned by centuries of moral repression. They are grey forces which foster blinding ignorance in our lives. As a result, men are either ascetic or complete sexual hedonists. The Christ-force would eliminate all past moral teachings and have us do what we want in regard to sexuality without guilt or blame. The Christ-force would have us follow our own emotional reactions and find harmony.[80]

Fear is beneficial, according to Process. Fear is the catalyst which drives us out of the grey way of ignorance and neutrality into action. Fear is the energizer which causes a person to brush aside the bitterness of failure and push forward to new heights.[81]

In the present corrupt world, grey forces are becoming more and more dominant. The Puritans and Protestors will intensify their battles. The imminent end will sweep the loveless and ignorant grey characters away. Then the Christ-power in mankind will rise to dominance. One urgent task of the Process Church is to warn people of the impending end and the oncoming violent Armageddon. All but the few who are members of Process will be destroyed. Groups like the Hell's Angels, a California motorcycle gang, will be the troops of the last days. Process, as did Charles Manson, actively sought to solicit the Hells' Angels to its side.[82]

Process and Charles Manson. Although the accusation continues to be a disputed point, Bugliosi in *Helter Skelter* makes a strong case for the influence of Process teaching on Manson. We have already mentioned that Manson and his family lived only two blocks from Process headquarters in San Francisco in 1967 and 1968. There is fairly persuasive evidence that Manson borrowed some of the Process teachings. Both Process and Manson preached an imminent, violent Armageddon, basing their idea on the book of Revelation. Both saw the motorcycle gangs as troops of the last day. Both unified Satan and Christ. Manson was known to his followers as both Satan and Christ. The idea of fear held by Process and Manson is almost identical. The idea of "the family" was used by both Process and Manson up to 1969. The Process symbol is similar to the one Manson carved on his forehead. These similarities and contacts convinced Bugliosi that Manson borrowed heavily from Process.[83]

Process is quick to point out differences from Manson. For one thing, they decry violence. It is also true that Manson was influenced by other groups such as the Solar Lodge of the Ordo Temple Orientis, a magical cult specializing in blood drinking and sex magic.[84]

Regional headquarters for Process are presently established in Boston, New York, Chicago, San Francisco, New Orleans, and Miami. A beautifully produced magazine called *The Process* is printed simultaneously in these cities.

Local branches of the Process church have ascending steps of membership. An applicant is called an acolyte. The next step, the initiate, involves baptism with fire and water and a cross presentation. At this level, ascription is made to a covenant between Christ and Satan. Disciple of the unity is the next level of membership. At this level a person is given a new name and accepted into the unity of Christ and Satan. A full-time worker is called a messenger of unity. On a still higher level is an inside processean or a prophet. The apex is to be a part of the eleven-member council that advises the "Oracle" and Founder, Robert de Grimston.[85]

Since the Process seeks to unite intellect and emotion, much is made of ritual utilizing a distinctive, electronic type of music and original liturgies and chants. Services are held every night. They feature healing, dramatics, meditation, chanting, and forums. The sabbath service uses candles, charts, and incense. Both the Christian cross and the satanic goat symbol adorn the altar during worship. Psychic powers are sought and taught.[86]

THEOLOGICAL EVALUATION OF PROCESS

It is obvious that Process reflects a pantheistic doctrine in which all opposites are transcended. All things are ultimately fused into one. All is one and one is all. In this one all the opposites, including good and evil, are eternally reconciled. A person can be both Christ and Satan.[87]

The curse of mankind, for Process, is to have a sense of guilt or assign blame. In blaming the Christian churches for creating guilt and shame, Process often distorts and caricatures authentic Christian teachings.

The Christian perspective teaches that the world is the creation of a holy and transcendent God. Man is made in God's image. God knows what will bring man fulfillment and happiness. Man has revolted and lost his way but, without destroying our freedom, God has sent help in and through Israel and Jesus Christ. In the person of Christ and in the biblical teaching, eternal principles of right and wrong are revealed.

R. C. Zaehner maintains that the loss of the biblical standards plus the acceptance of the teaching of groups like Process help account for developments like the Manson Family. For Zaehner the teachings of Process constitute a deadly poison.[88]

3
The Jesus People and the New Consciousness Emphases

The Unification Church and Process are obviously distortions of classical Christianity. In recent years, however, the more normative Christian churches have become interested in what can be construed as N.C. interests. For example, the most dynamic development in Christianity in this decade has been the neocharismatic renewal. This emphasis on the Spirit-filled life, speaking in tongues, and other spiritual gifts is even more widespread in Catholic circles than in the Protestant churches. A Roman Catholic leader has suggested that the occasion of the neocharismatic renewal is the failure of the churches to meet the deep emotional needs of the human spirit. The strengths and weaknesses of this phase of the N.C. outbreak are outside the limits of our study.[89]

Another Christian development which has N.C. implications relates to the Jesus People. The Jesus movement began in the late 1960s. I was lecturing and teaching in San Francisco and Los Angeles as the Jesus movement took form. It reached such proportions that in 1971 the Jesus People movement constituted the religious news story of the year, appearing on the covers of both *Time* and *Newsweek*. The Jesus movement is characterized by a number of emphases, such as eschatology (Jesus is coming soon), apostasy (mainline churches are religious harlots), and "Jesus is one of us." The emphasis with which we are chiefly concerned, however, is experience. Enroth contends that the Jesus People, at least in the earlier days of the movement, were overwhelmingly and almost exclusively experience-oriented. Reason and a sense of history had little place in the Jesus movement.[90]

Berkeley, California, was one of the key Jesus centers. As I stood on Sproul Plaza on the University of California campus, at Berkeley, and watched the Jesus People perform, this antirationalist emphasis seemed ironic. The University of California had just been judged the number one graduate school (rationalistic center) in the nation. Coming out of the drug scene and the occult world, as many Jesus People did, the words *trip*, *high*, and *turned-on* were widely used. These experience-oriented words were now used, however, in relation to Jesus. Many of us remember a favorite phrase of the Jesus People, "After Jesus, everything else is toothpaste." The former druggies were now getting a new consciousness high in Christianity.[91]

It will be of interest to note that some of the more far-out Jesus groups utilized consciousness-altering techniques similar to those we have found in Hindu, Buddhist, and Islamic-related groups. Martin Marty contends that the Eastern N.C. techniques have transfused and transformed the Western religious tradition. The Jesus People, says Marty, are telling us that Christianity is acceptable again with an altered style of consciousness.[92] A brief statement of these N.C. techniques will help relate certain emphases of the Jesus People to the major groups we have studied.

THE LOCAL CHURCH (WITNESS LEE)

In one sense, The Local Church is not a Jesus group. It has been assimilated and copied, however, by the Jesus People. The Local Church roots are in the Little Flock movement of Watchman Nee of China. Witness Lee, a Nee follower, took the Little Flock movement to Taiwan and on to the United States as the Communists gained ground in China. In 1962 Witness Lee took over sole leadership of The Local Church group in the United States.

The Local Church has many unique emphases. It teaches that there is to be one church for one city—The Local Church. Denominations are abominable—they are called whores. Our particular interest is in the N.C. techniques employed by The Local Church. Like Hare Krishna, Nicheren Shoshu, and Transcendental Meditation, they use a mantra or chant. Unbelievers are urged to chant "O Lord" three times in order to be saved. "O Lord Jesus" is repeated constantly by The Local Church members—up to a thousand times a day. The members are taught to "breathe in" God and exhale the four syllables "O Lord Jesus." The congregation is told to "get out of your mind," quit thinking, and repeat "O Lord Jesus." [93]

Another emphasis in The Local Church is called *pray-read*. Members are told not to think as they pray-read. Instead they are to read the Bible and respond with whatever enters their spirits. Second Timothy 3:16 states that all Scripture is God breathed. Witness Lee states that this means that, "All Scripture is God's breath." Since God is spirit, God's breath is spirit. Therefore to pray-read the Bible is to eat and drink spiritually of God's nature and essence. The Bible is the very essence of God, instead of the revelation of God. The Bible is also the essence of Christ himself. The Bible and Christ are the same.[94] This view is similar in many ways to the Islamic view of the Koran.

In many ways, the emphases of The Local Church remind us of some of the practices of Hare Krishna and Nicheren Shoshu. For example, to repeat the *Lotus Sutra* of Nicheren is to partake of the Buddha spirit itself.

THE WAY

Victor Paul Wierville, founder of The Way, was once a straight United Church of Christ minister who had a Princeton theology degree. One day, in disgust, he threw his three thousand theological books in the city dump and decided to read only the Bible. In 1953, after six years of prayer, Wierville claims that the power and revelation of God came upon him. Within five years, by 1968, his new movement, called The Way, was going full steam ahead with WOW (Word over the World) ambassadors working at home and abroad.[95]

Many of Wierville's teachings are heretical by classical Christian standards. For example, God is seen as one in being and one in person (no Trinity). Jesus Christ is not coeternal with God.[96] The Holy Spirit is just another name for God. There is, however, a human holy spirit (small *h*). A Christian is to be filled with holy spirit (not "the" Holy Spirit).[97] In the fall, Adam had his spirit taken away from him. To reverse this, the Christian is given the gift of holy spirit which is a matter of certain spiritual abilities such as speaking in tongues, prophecy, and healing. The human holy spirit produces true worship by causing a person to speak in tongues. All Way people must speak in tongues out loud and in their heads. An almost mechanical method has been worked out for *everyone* to speak in tongues. The only true worship is speaking in tongues. Many followers speak in tongues for hours a day to strengthen their spiritual faculties and meet their problems. Thinking is to be subordinate to this constant speaking in tongues.[98]

It is obvious that Wierville's teaching about the holy spirit is far different from that of classical Christianity or the neocharismatic movement. Instead, The Way resembles the innate or inherent power of consciousness idea which is prominent in Eastern N.C. groups.[99]

THE LOVE FAMILY (THE CHURCH OF ARMAGEDDON)

The Love Family was founded in 1969 in Seattle, Washington, by Love Israel (formerly Paul Erdman). The Love Family has many typical Jesus People emphases. Important for our study is its emphasis on drugs, breathing, and electrical shocks.

In addition to consciousness heightening through ecstatic singing and dancing, the Love Family uses marijuana, dried mushrooms, and hashish to induce religious ecstasy. Until two young members were asphyxiated in their services, they inhaled toluene, an industrial solvent, as a religious ritual. Today they employ hyperventilating through rapid, deep breathing as a part of their worship. They also use electrical shocks to heighten religious consciousness.[100]

THE ALAMO CHRISTIAN FOUNDATION

One of the original Jesus groups is the Alamo Christian Foundation, founded by Tony and Susan Alamo. Although primarily communal and apocalyptic (Jesus is coming soon) in nature, some N.C. techniques are utilized. Fasting is encouraged. Their services are characterized by constant chanting and praising. Sensory deprivation is induced through limited food and limited sleep.[101]

THE HOLY ORDER OF MANS

One of the newest spiritual groups, made up mostly of young Jesus People types, is the Holy Order of MANS. It was founded in 1968 by Earl Blighton, a sixty-five-year-old ex-engineer, who claims to have received a divine revelation about the founding of the order. Terms utilized in their literature, such as *esoteric council, the God-being,* and *realization of the God-self* indicate that they are closely akin to Hindu groups we have studied. Another classical occult and Eastern influence on their teaching is seen in their designation of Jesus as a great teacher who attained contact with a Christ-consciousness. Jesus is separated from Christ and thus from his uniqueness as Savior and Messiah.[102]

The Holy Order also emphasizes reincarnation and an illumination service. In the illumination service, light or a vibration of energy is received into the personality. This light service opens the self to the point of god within oneself.[103] The Spiritual Counterfeits Project contends that the Holy Order of MANS is deliberately designed to put a Christian gloss on a non-Christian movement.[104]

THE CHRISTIAN WORLD LIBERATION FRONT

In the late 1960s and early 1970s I had a fellowship with key leaders of the Christian World Liberation Front in San Francisco. I agree with Enroth that this group and its auxiliaries constitute one of the most constructive continuing facets of the Jesus Movement.[105] It has shown both intellectual and spiritual maturity. Its paper, *Right On,* incorporated into *Radix,* is contemporary and intelligent. In this group, a rare combination of intensive spiritual turn on, intellectual awareness, and social concern is manifested. The Christian World Liberation Front has been a revitalization movement in the midst of more traditional churches.[106]

PART SIX
Occult-related New Consciousness Emphases
(Sorcery, Drugs, and Magic)

One of the most dramatic traditions in human history is the story of the Indians migrating from Asia across the Bering Strait to North America. Although details are disputed, the consensus is that they made their way across what is now Canada, into the United States, and then into Mexico, and Central and South America. Through the centuries the Indians have reflected and developed a world of sorcery, magic, and unique consciousness techniques.

In the National Anthropological Museum in Mexico City, one is overwhelmed by the displays of both ancient and contemporary Indian life. What is this world of beliefs where sorcery and magic are practiced? How do their N.C. techniques compare with those of the Hindu, Buddhist, and Islamic groups which we have explored? How are the American Indian teachings related to the recent magic and witchcraft practices which have become prominent in Western Europe and in North America? What are the N.C. techniques employed by the sorcerers of the American Indian life?

A major doorway into this American Indian N.C. world has been opened by a transplanted Peruvian, Carlos Castaneda. For twelve years, as an anthropology student, he apprenticed himself to Don Juan, a Yaqui Indian sorcerer or magician. Castaneda has written five books telling about his experiences. These books, selling more than a half a million copies, have become international best sellers.[1]

Castaneda describes in a powerful and compelling way a view of reality which is separate from the normal Western view. He further reveals the techniques of attaining this new perspective or new consciousness. In fact, Carlos Castaneda has become a hero for people concerned with new ways of expanding consciousness and viewing reality.

There is one basic difference between Castaneda and the other N.C. representatives we have studied. He apparently has no desire to be a N.C. guru, found an organization or group, or work out fixed meditation or occult techniques.[2] This lack of cultic ambition is in contrast to the work of European and North American magic and witchcraft gurus, such as Anton La Vey and his Church of Satan.

1
Castaneda and Don Juan—Their Background and Dialogue

CASTANEDA—LIFE AND BACKGROUND

A stocky, affable Latin, seldom photographed, Castaneda was born in Peru in 1925 of humble parents. (Until *Time* exposed his biographical distortions, he claimed to have been born of elite parents in Brazil in 1935.) Moving to Lima, Peru, he studied art and was known to his schoolmates as a witty, imaginative fellow who was a big liar. In 1951, he fulfilled a long-held obsession to come to the United States. He is now an American citizen.[3]

In 1960, as an ambitious young student, Castaneda made plans to enter graduate school at the University of California at Los Angeles. To assure acceptance and gain a head start as a graduate student, he decided to do a study on medicinal and psychotropic plants used by the Yaqui Indians. This was to lead him to the sorcerer Don Juan and twelve years of an off-and-on apprenticeship.[4] His wife, after their divorce, reports that he had an intense interest in occultism before he met Don Juan.[5]

The twelve years of reported field work with the Mexican shaman, or sorcerer, Don Juan, eventually formed the basis for five books which have sold hundreds of thousands of copies and made Castaneda a wealthy man. The work with Don Juan also led to the M.A. and Ph.D. degrees from U.C.L.A. and international recognition.

The normally talkative "bull-shooter" Castaneda now lives in Los Angeles as a recluse. He seldom lectures or appears in public. After the off-and-on years with Don Juan in the desert and in border towns, Castaneda seems to have had reentry problems. He lives a totally irregular and mysterious life.[6]

DON JUAN—LIFE AND BACKGROUND

Apparently no American other than Castaneda has met Don Juan. Castaneda asserts that Don Juan was born in Mexico in 1891. The pseudonym Juan Matus or Don Juan has been given to the sorcerer to protect his privacy. Don Juan suffered through constant forced movement and wandering as a young man. His parents were murdered by soldiers, and he was consequently further isolated from normal home ties. Wandering from place to place in Mexico, he absorbed the occult beliefs of various Indian tribes.[7]

Don Juan called himself a *brujo*, or "man of knowledge." These terms refer to what anthropologists call a sorcerer, shaman, or magician.

THE RELATIONSHIP OF CASTANEDA AND DON JUAN

As already mentioned, Castaneda was planning to go to graduate school at U.C.L.A. and study anthropology. He was advised that the preparation of a short paper on ethnobotany involving a study of the use of psychotropic plants used by the Yaqui Indians would give him a head start. At a friend's suggestion, he contacted an old Indian man who was said to know about peyote and medicinal plants. This was Don Juan. He met Don Juan in a dusty Arizona bus depot near the Mexican border.[8]

First stage: 1961-65. After their initial encounter, other visits between Castaneda and Don Juan were rather frequent. About a year later, in June of 1961, Don Juan decided to pass on to Castaneda the knowledge of sorcery and magic which he had himself learned from his teacher.[9]

According to Castaneda's account, the first phase of his apprenticeship to Don Juan lasted from 1961 to 1965. When he finally became terrified by his experiences, Castaneda broke away from Don Juan, in 1965. Utilizing his thousands of pages of notes, Castaneda described the first stage of his epic training in *The Teachings of Don Juan: A Yaqui Way of Knowledge.* The book was written for his U.C.L.A. master's thesis and was published in 1968 by the University of California Press. It soon moved out of the academic world and became a national best-seller.[10]

Second stage: 1968-72, In gratitude to Don Juan, Castaneda in 1968 went down to Mexico again to give the old wizard a copy of *The Teachings of Don Juan.* A second cycle of instruction began. As a result of this advanced teaching, Castaneda was able to write his second book, *A Separate Reality.* It was published in 1971. It is a sequel to *The Teachings of Don Juan.* In this book, we are told that Don Juan insisted on the necessity of Castaneda's breaking through to the ultimate goal of learning to see by his own efforts.[11]

Journey to Ixtlan: The Lessons of Don Juan published in 1972, is not a sequel to the first two books except for the last three of its twenty chapters. In these last three chapters of *Ixtlan*, Castaneda describes the experiences which gave him a new sense of his relationship to Don Juan's world. Because of this new understanding Castaneda sees the true significance of the lessons which Don Juan had given him in earlier years. In *Journey to Ixtlan* these lessons are clearly outlined. *Ixtlan* was used as Castaneda's thesis for his Ph.D. degree in anthropology at U.C.L.A.[12]

Third stage: 1972-74. The next teaching given to Castaneda by Don Juan is recorded in *Tales of Power,* published in 1974. *Tales* is based on experiences which Castaneda had with Don Juan in 1971 and 1972. The experiences described in *Tales* start a few months after those recounted in *Ixtlan. Tales* tell of Carlos Castaneda as an advanced student. Descriptions are given of techniques for full initiation into sorcery. Comprehensive explanations are given for the strategies used throughout the eleven or twelve years of Castaneda's apprenticeship.[13] A more recent book is *The Second Ring of Power* (1977).

CASTANEDA AND CONTINUING CONTROVERSY

From the beginning, Castaneda and his work have been controversial. U.C.L.A. sociology professor Harold Garfinkel gave Castaneda's work harsh criticism. Living off odd jobs as a taxi driver and delivery boy, Castaneda rewrote *The Teachings of Don Juan* three times before it was accepted as his master's thesis.[14]

By the time *Journey to Ixtlan* was published in 1972, criticism about the authenticity of the conversations with Don Juan and even the historicity of Don Juan were rampant. Readers scoured the Southwest looking for signs of Don Juan without success.[15]

Anthropologists contend that Don Juan does not reflect the true Yaqui Indian way of life. A Mexican ethnologist states that he feels that Castaneda's works have a very high percentage of imagination. Literary scholars such as Joyce Carol Oates have joined the criticism. Some suggest that Castaneda's writings are based on the style of Argentinian Jurge Luis Borges. Richard de Mille, in his book *Castaneda's Journey,* contends that the books of Castaneda are some kind of semi-spoof or skillful fiction. De Mille further states that Castaneda's professors eventually recognized that they had been hoaxed. Nevertheless, to prevent embarrassment of U.C.L.A. and themselves, they proceeded to award him a doctorate. Others say that Don Juan may be a composite Indian.[16]

In rereading the works of Castaneda, I gained the impression that they were almost too clever and sophisticated to be literally true reports of a formally uneducated sorcerer's words and ideas. Castaneda himself admits that the books are obviously in his own words but that they are true reflections of Don Juan's teachings. In any case, Castaneda's books unfold with clarity and narrative power the world of the shaman in a way unmatched in other anthropological studies. These books are dramatic presentations of the age-old techniques of sorcery, drugs, magic, and witchcraft.

2
Castaneda and the Chief Emphases of the Occult-related New Consciousness View

Castaneda's writings describe in a graphic form the chief emphases of one of mankind's oldest N.C. views—the occult. A further contribution of Castaneda's work is his description of the way in which he changed from a typical, rational Western man to a person with occult understanding. He not only understood but he also tells how he eventually became a participant in the occult world. It will be helpful to outline Castaneda's statement of occult emphases and relate them to contemporary N.C. developments.

There is a separate occult world of reality which is accessible to rational, Western man through certain ancient mind-altering techniques.

The Western rational tradition comes to us culturally determined and packaged in advance.[17] What we take as reality and as rationally possible is determined by consensus or by a social contract. Anthropology deals with different descriptions of reality. Primitive people, in fact, have many separate realities. As an anthropologist, Castaneda decided to study the perspective on reality of a Mexican sorcerer, Don Juan. To do this, he spent years learning the techniques of entering into this different occult mode of seeing life and reality. In order to get into another man's consensus of reality, according to Castaneda, one's own view must be temporarily or permanently broken up. This is a most difficult undertaking. Few Westerners, for various reasons, will attempt such a venture. A guide is needed, and in the case of Castaneda, Don Juan was willing and available.[18]

The invisible universe which Don Juan describes is a reality beyond the visible universe. The visible universe is one to which we all have access through the five senses and which operates according to the so-called "laws of nature" discovered by natural science. This acceptance of the visible or material universe on the part of the modern-day representatives of the occult view makes it different from the Hindu and Buddhist perspectives. As we discussed earlier, the Hindu and Buddhist groups tend to say that this ordinary, eternal world is ultimately illusion although usable for secondary purposes.[19]

All of us are acquainted with the visible world. We perceive it through ordinary consciousness or straight thinking. Space is understood as stretched out in three dimensions. The same space cannot be occupied by two bodies at the same time. Time is seen as linear—there is a past, present, and future. Standards of good and evil are accepted.[20]

Beyond the visible world, according to Don Juan, is another world which is called a "separate reality." The particular version of reality which Don Juan represents is related to animism. It is also known as the sorcery or shamanistic tradition. It is the general view of life that underlies primitive or so-called pagan religions. As we will see, this view is not simple but is a highly complex system. It is a prelogical view of reality that is no-one-knows-how old.[21]

There are certain ideas in the occult tradition that we see reflected in Don Juan's teachings.

The universe is filled with countless spiritual beings who are arranged in a certain hierarchical way according to their power. Although there is often a high god at the top, he has little personal interest in man. These spiritual powers can interact with humans.[22]

These numerous spiritual beings vary in temperament from the vicious to the comic and helpful. A successful sorcerer must eventually obtain the help of an ally or guardian spirit.

The only way to survive in life is to learn how to placate or buy off the evil spirits and get the help of the good spirits. The world of sorcery, magic, and witchcraft is thus concerned with gifts, offerings, rituals, and incantations that affect the spirits. Related to the occult view are the worlds of white magic (getting the help of the good spirits) and black magic (enlisting the evil spirits to harm others).[23]

Sorcerers, such as Don Juan, are variously called shamans, magicians, or witch doctors. Through a special call and long strenuous training, the sorcerer learns to control the spirit world, at least to a large extent.[24]

Ordinary people are dependent on the sorcerer's power to help them get through life and keep away the evil spirits. The heart of magic is the discovery of how to manipulate the universal powers or forces of the universe. The sorcerer is theoretically an expert in the power field.

The world is seen as a great unity. Spirit and matter occupy the same continuum. The spiritual distinction between men and animals as made in the Bible is not present. Animals are seen as the direct ancestors of man. It is possible for people to change into animals. Trees and plants, as well as animals, are seen as containing souls.[25]

Once Castaneda claims that he became a crow and flew off with three other crows on a three-day trip. He also reports a conversation with a coyote. In the conversation the coyote, when asked how he was doing, replied, "I am doing fine. How about you?" Castaneda admits that he did not hear the coyote in a normal way. He claims, however, that his body knew what the coyote was saying. His body automatically translated into words the feeling which the animal was communicating. In the magical mode of consciousness, it seems as if the whole world is alive and that human beings are in a communion that includes animals and plants.[26]

A number of contemporary people interested in the N.C. developments tell of talking to, loving, and praying for plants. Positive results are reported. John Lilly, a prominent scientist interested in N.C. developments, reports that he communicates with dolphins.[27]

Most sophisticated N.C. advocates will not accept without modifications all of the teachings and beliefs of the world of sorcery. These modern-day occultists will often demythologize magic by utilizing psychological concepts or by giving it a naturalistic twist. Nevertheless, most of them will admit that their view has roots in animism and in the ancient world of the occult. These contemporary occultists often look to Eastern or Western sorcerers or magicians for many of their ideas. Theodore Roszak, a sophisticated California professor and occultist, openly calls for a return to the "old Gnosis" of the ancient magicians and sorcerers. Man's hope, he affirms, is in synthesizing and using their techniques.[28]

It is important to have the presence of a guide during early attempts to see a separate reality. In the world of sorcery, one sees only through the help of a person who has already seen it. The guide is analagous to the guru or perfect master in the Hindu-related N.C. groups.[29]

Induction into the occult world is not like the quick course in ceremonial magic or witchcraft held in the evenings in local occult book stores. Induction should be very gradual, said Don Juan, and accompanied by patience and restraint.[30]

The guide must first help you to break the certainty that the world is the way you have been taught. He seeks to help you strip yourself of the explanations and assumptions that shape and limit your vision. After you have been stripped of your limited perspective, the guide shows you the new reality of sorcery. A subsequent step has the guide teaching you how it is possible to hold both the old and new worlds of reality together. A further step is when you are brought to the realization that neither the old nor the new view is a final view. A difficult but important step is to learn how to slip between the two descriptions and stop the world and see. You are left with the wonder of seeing the world without interpretation. Don Juan's system of stopping the world is finally explained in *Journey to Ixtlan.*[31]

154

It is obvious to those trained in philosophy that Castaneda has drawn on the European philosophical movement of phenomenology, initiated by Edmund Husserl, to explain Don Juan's teaching. According to the phenomenologists, what we perceive as reality depends on the interpretation we have been led to place on an ultimately mysterious universe. If we can bracket out our normal ways of perceiving the world, we can see how arbitrary previous interpretations are. The thrust of Don Juan's teaching is to break down Castaneda's conviction that the ordinary world with its limits is the only field of human experience. The eventual goal, at least for the strong and brave, is to obtain a new view of reality and a new set of interpretations. As taught by Don Juan, this new view will permit the sorcerer to perform superhuman feats such as changing his human form.[32]

According to Castaneda, Don Juan led him to participate in some of these new areas. Castaneda reports some out-of-this-world experiences. This new world discovered by Carlos Castaneda is not just an extension of known physical laws but a separate reality.[33]

In the writings of Castaneda, we are offered tantalizing glimpses into a world that is off limits to most people. It is off limits because most of us have been told that it does not exist. Don Juan tells us through Castaneda that the separate reality does exist and offers great rewards to those who can enter. He warns, however, of the incredible danger of such a trip when it is taken casually or without proper guidance.[34]

Natural drugs (psychotropic plants) are valuable for some people as an initiatory vehicle into the separate reality or new consciousness.

As we have seen, the first step in moving into a new reality is bracketing out old views and presuppositions. Castaneda was a tough case so Don Juan resorted to natural drugs (psychotropic plants) to help him in this initial process of bracketing. Momentarily the drugs wiped out Castaneda's isolated ego.[35]

The Teachings of Don Juan describe the way in which natural drugs were used in the initiation. Preparations made from three well-known plants, Peyote cactus, Jimson weed, and a species of mushroon were ingested under Don Juan's careful control and interpretation. Castaneda stated that the drugs produced in him peculiar states of distorted perception and altered consciousness. After chewing peyote buttons, he reported that he met Mescalito, the personified power of peyote, as a black dog, a singing light, and as a cricket with a green head. He talked with a coyote after smoking mushroom dust. He also reported seeing a guardian spirit rise before him as a one hundred-foot-high gnat. After rubbing his body with a datura ointment, Castaneda experienced the sensation of flying.[36]

Don Juan and Castaneda discount drugs. In Castaneda's third and probably most significant book, *Journey to Ixtlan,* a change of viewpoint on drugs is given. He reversed the impression given in *Teachings* and *Separate Reality* that the use of natural drugs was the main method Don Juan intended to use in bringing him to see the separate reality. He stated that Don Juan only used psychotropic plants in the earlier days of his apprenticeship because of his stupidity and bullheadedness. The natural drugs helped to shatter the dogmatic idea that the rational view of reality is the only view. For Castaneda, the price he paid for taking drugs was extensive. The drugs weakened his body and it took months for him to recuperate.[37]

Don Juan himself does not use natural drugs regularly. He states that when he acts responsibly, and properly uses other techniques, drugs are not needed.

In 1964 Carlos Castaneda was invited to an East Village party in New York City which was attended by such luminaries as Timothy Leary. Under drug influence, Castaneda reported that the party goers were like silly children indulging in incoherent revelations. He was disgusted with the acid heads. He stated that an authentic sorcerer takes drugs for a different reason than do the acid heads. Drugs are only a means to an end. As ends in themselves, drugs are pathologically regressive and spiritually stultifying. Castaneda further suggested that Timothy Leary was only improvising in his drug-taking from within his Western view and merely rearranging old perspectives. There was no authentic breakthrough for Leary, according to Castaneda.[38]

The negative statements by Carlos Castaneda on drugs came as quite a shock to many of his psychedelic admirers. They thought he would be stoned most of the time. The psychedelic crowd wanted him to tell them to turn on and blow their minds. These drug devotees were further upset when they learned that he does not smoke, drink hard liquor, or even use marijuana. In fact, Castaneda reports that his only drug experiences took place under the careful guidance of Don Juan.[39]

The teachings of Don Juan and the writings of Castaneda have implications for America's drug-oriented society. It is true that natural drugs have been used to induce states of mystical consciousness for centuries. Greek mystery cults as well as religious groups in Siberia and South America have used materials produced from hemp, datura, henbane, and mushroom. John M. Allegro, in his book *Sacred Mushrooms and the Cross,* argues that the stories of the Old Testament and the New Testament reflect a drug and fertility cult that utilized a hallucinogenic mushroom. He even goes so far as to say that the New Testament books were coded initiations into the secrets of the cult. There is little evidence for Allegro's thesis.[40] Indians in Mexico and the United States have had legalization for the use of peyote in carefully supervised religious services. More recently synthetic derivatives such as LSD and Mescaline have been used for mystical and religious purposes.

Drugs and mysticism. In 1954 Aldous Huxley in his *Doors of Perception* told of undergoing a mystical experience, induced by mescaline which united him with ultimate reality. In the 1960s, at Harvard, Timothy Leary and Richard Alpert argued for the place of psychedelics in consciousness raising. Groups such as the Beatles followed by other psychedelic music groups, popularized drugs in the rapidly expanding counterculture.

In 1957, the prominent Oxford scholar, R. C. Zaehner wrote *Mysticism Sacred and Profane.* In this book he challenged the teaching of Aldous Huxley that there was a positive relationship between drugs and Christian mysticism. Zaehner asserts that it is an absurd arrogance to state that a mescaline drug high is the same as an authentic Christian mystical experience. According to Zaehner, psychedelic experiences may have some similarity to a nontheistic, monistic mysticism. The characteristics of monistic mysticism include cosmic oneness, transcendence of space and time, feelings of well-being, and increased sensory perception of color and sound. This type of mysticism is not in the biblical tradition but, as we have seen, more appropriate to India.[41]

The Christian mystic would say that any mystical absorption restricted to one's self or with nature falls short of biblical mysticism. The idea of a world force or an absolute is not the same as belief in a personal God.

Christian mysticism. From the perspective of classical Christianity, nothing can displace the concrete historical figure of Jesus Christ from the central place in religious experience. In an authentic Christian mysticism there is a mutual abiding of Christ and the Father and the Christian disciple. Although there is personal fellowship, the biblical faith will not allow complete union and identification of the creature with the Creator (man with God). Individuality is heightened in Christian mysticism, not minimized.

Christian mysticism also seeks a balance between contemplation and ethical action. Such a mysticism is best engendered in a setting such as church, a Christian retreat, or a home. Physical worship aids may help the practice of Christian mysticism, but it is dependent for its origination and consummation on God's initiative and upholding power.[42]

Man is a mystical creature. He wants to heighten his consciousness. From the Christian perspective, man must be led beyond drugs. In the words of Augustine, the famous fifth-century Christian mystic, "Thou hast made us for Thyself, O Lord, and we are restless until we rest in thee."

There are various non-drug-related techniques which are useful in the quest to see the separate reality. Don Juan taught Carlos Castaneda some occult techniques and abilities for consciousness raising that are very, very old. According to Don Juan the apprentice must follow them closely. A brief list will give some indication of the type of techniques used.

A. Erase personal history and sentiment. An apprentice should be inaccessible and elusive.

B. Create a fog around yourself. Free yourself of daily routines which dull perception. Castaneda states that he still disrupts his routine in order to catch new perspectives.[43]

C. Remind yourself constantly of death. When death becomes a reality for you, you will be able to make changes more easily, become more decisive, and be less governed by the expectations of others and by the ordinary social routines. A spiritual warrior must live as if this is the last moment or the last battle. Nothing should be left pending. There are no large and small decisions, only decisions that must be made now. And there is no time for doubts and regret.[44] Similar ideas are taught by the German philosopher, Martin Heidegger.

A unique emphasis in sorcery, however, is that death is a physical, shadowlike presence that can be felt and seen. Death stands to your left and is an impartial judge which speaks the truth to you. The moment you remember that you must eventually die you are cut down to the right size.[45]

D. Develop a total body awareness. The Western mind sees the world as built largely from what the eyes report to the mind. We see a world out there and talk to our eyes about it. We are here and the world is there. Our eyes feed on reason. In sorcery, the total body is used as a preceptor. Western man assumes that subject and object are separated. In sorcery, the body is already in the world. You just tune in and train your body to make it a good receptor. For the sorcerer, the body is not an object to be filled with alcohol, bad food, and anxiety. Western man thinks that germs invade the body from the outside. Our answer is to impart medicine to cure the body. The disease is not a part of us. Don Juan, to the contrary, teaches that disease is a disharmony between man and the world.[46]

E. According to sorcery, we are to stop thinking and incessantly talking. Cease the internal mental chatter. Stop being chained to reason. Don't think but look, stretch forth, and see. The world is beyond reason and demands new modes of thinking.[47]

In contemporary N.C. circles a similar idea is seen in the emphasis on left-handed thinking. According to some writers, the left side of the brain relates to intuition, dreams, feeling, and the wisdom of the body.[48]

F. Develop ability to control in a voluntary way your dream images. Don Juan taught that this can be done by sustaining dream images long enough to look at them carefully. He suggested that you use your hands as a steady point and go back and forth between them and the dream images. Castaneda learned to find his hands and stop the dream. Related to dream control is the use of dreams to find lost articles and the development of techniques to go on out-of-the-body journeys during sleep.[49]

The full use of magical power can only be acquired with the help of an ally or a spirit entity.

When the basic lessons of sorcery have been mastered, when the apprentice begins finally to reach toward his goal, he will encounter an ally or spirit entity. This ally will challenge the apprentice. At this stage, many apprentices back out. If a person wrestles and loses he will be snuffed out—either literally or figuratively. To win, a person must continue meditative practices and utilize occult techniques that will identify him with the positive forces that guide the universe. This meditation must be done with minute attention to detail. If you win, the reward is true power.[50]

Don Juan and the occult perspective think of these allies which are perceived in states of altered consciousness as having existence apart from the conscious self. On a different level, the Christian sees the Holy Spirit, his ally, as having personality and ontological or metaphysical existence.

The idea of spirit beings still persists in our culture. In recent days a torrent of books have developed the theme that the gods and demons of ancient cults were in fact astronauts who came from more highly evolved civilizations on other planets. I heard Erich von Däniken give an unbelievable lecture on the subject of his book, *Chariots of the Gods?* Von Däniken gave detailed illustrations from various cultures as evidence that the ancient world was familiar with the appearances of spaceships and astronauts. Pictures were shown of archeological remains which he said were built to serve as guideposts for space travelers. For Von Däniken, the spiritual ally, then, is only the distorted recollection of a superior technology. Someone is out there and the reports of flying saucers may be an indication that these beings will come again.[51]

Carl Jung sees the images of men in capsules or in space helmets as arising out of our collective unconsciousness. These spacemen constitute an objectification of human images. This view permits the skeptics to accept the occurrence of a paranormal events and still maintain a naturalistic framework.[52]

Both Jung and von Däniken would then say that there is nothing really supernatural out there. For the occultist, however, the spiritual ally is a spiritual being who is quite independent of the human imagination. Even if there was a superior technology involved in the construction of such an architectural wonder as the pyramids, those who possessed the technical ability were still spiritual beings.[53]

The final purpose of taking an apprenticeship is the ancient desire to know and to learn how to control the mysterious forces of the universe. One who really knows and can manipulate the universal forces is called a warrior.

Through the years Castaneda has equivocated on the matter of having a final battle with an ally and becoming a warrior. Recent statements indicate that he may go deeper into sorcery and take the dangerous step.[54]

Perhaps the danger of being a warrior is a part of the explanation of the contemporary interest in Don Juan. In a time of cultural breakdown, there is a renewed interest in the story of an amoral man of knowledge and power.[55] The implication of the accounts of Don Juan is that he can call upon and use strange powers to see, know, and transform the world.

Sorcery and magic are primarily related to man's desire to understand and control the universal forces. Both white and black magic are related to power. Through the centuries, as we have seen, techniques, formulas, and rituals designed to channel and use magic powers have been developed and passed on. Even today ritual magic, the magic circle, and the summoning of the spirits are widely practiced in highly educated parts of the world such as the United States and Europe.

Younger occultists, such as Anton La Vey (Church of Satan) and Philip Bonewits (who received the first degree in magic from the University of California) see magic as related to psychic dimensions rather than supernatural forces. Other contemporary magicians, like Don Juan, believe in the metaphysical reality of the spirits. For David Farren, magic's lack of moral content, apart from a crude hedonism, is a point of great concern.[56]

The Bible recognizes the reality of the occult world. But since the time that God's people moved into Canaan, (a land of many sorcerers and much magic), the prophets, Jesus Christ, and biblical leaders have opposed magic. Contemporary magic is in the pagan tradition. Wayne Oates points out that current magicians, instead of bringing their powers into a consecrated relationship to God, are using them in alienation from God as a means of self-aggrandizement and cleverness.[57]

3
The Modern Response to the Occult World of Sorcery and Magic

Occult experiences like those of Carlos Castaneda are widely reported. How do moderns interpret them?

Some accept the ontological reality of the occult and spirit world. There are spiritual centers of consciousness other than God and man, they affirm. Such beings reside in a fifth dimension. In altered states of consciousness powers in this dimension can be contacted. This view is the oldest but least acceptable to most moderns. Trances and incantations are characteristic of this approach. The movies *The Exorcist* and *The Omen* illustrate this view.[58]

The psychedelic view is that the spirits are projections of the conscious self. The spiritual realities are spun out by the self when one is in an altered state of consciousness.[59]

The Conceptual Relativist view sees the spirit beings as forms or creations of thought—not true objects. If you test these spirits by any strict standard of objective truth, they will melt away into nothing. Although the spirits have no ontological reality, people who believe in them do produce a symbolic system.[60]

Naturalism would deny the reality of the occult world. Matter exists eternally and is all there is. Man is an interrelation of chemical and physical properties.[61]

The main thrust of the Bible is to establish in the mind of man the sole power and sovereignty of God and the importance of his Son, Jesus Christ, who revealed God's love, power, and purpose in history. The existence of the spirit world is affirmed. This world, however, is not on a par with God. It, like man, is a created order.

The existence of angels is mentioned in the Bible but hardly any reference is made as to how the Christian should contact angels or use them as guides. The chief emphasis of the Bible is on God and his Son, Jesus Christ, who constitute the source of man's power, knowledge, and salvation.[62]

Relatively little is said about Satan and demons in the Old Testament. When Christ appeared the veil was lifted and men were allowed to catch some glimpse of the negative world of the demonic. But even in the New

Testament there is no dualism. Satan and his demonic hosts were over-come in the cross and resurrection. They are active but have limitations. No spiritual beings are coequal with God or can overcome God and Jesus Christ. Christ has won the victory over the demonic powers in his cross and resurrection and in the coming of the Holy Spirit. The Christian is not forced to struggle with the demonic powers in his own strength.[63]

4
Secular Evaluations of the Occult-related New Consciousness Emphases

POSITIVE EVALUATION

The occult interest has opened up discussions about the limitations of the empirical and mechanistic views of man. The occult discussion has helped people to see that there is more than a one-dimensional perspective on life.[64]

NEGATIVE EVALUATION

The occult world is almost completely concerned with the inner con-sciousness of man. There seems to be little interest in the social structures that create alienation.[65]

5

Theological Evaluations

POSITIVE EVALUATIONS

A. Carlos Castaneda broke with the ordinary Western rational consensus with the help of Don Juan. He prepared the way for some people to look at alternative views including the Christian world view. We remember that Jesus Christ broke or modified the world consensus of ancient religious orthodoxies. Showing superiority over the occult view, Jesus Christ creates not only a new private world of fellowship with God but also creates a concern for others and for social justice.[66]

B. Don Juan reflects in a limited and distorted way many of the truths inherent in the Bible. These truths include the goodness and importance of the body and nature, the importance of seeing life in the light of death, and the place of the will and emotions as well as reason in spiritual knowledge. Instead of a spirit ally, the New Testament tells of the Holy Spirit, the third person in the Trinity, who lives within the Christian and guides, strengthens, and gives moral power.

NEGATIVE EVALUATIONS

A. The occult world teaches the existence of a sky god but he is removed and unconcerned and impersonal. From a Christian perspective, the existence of a personal, holy, and loving God—transcendent to man and yet involved with him—forms the basis for ethics and value judgments. The occult world has no such transcendent, personal, moral standard.[67]

B. As has already been indicated, demons and spirits continue to haunt the world of the occultist. Black magic and voodoo seek to employ the forces of the universe for evil purposes. Even if the spirits are called the projections of the psyche, they continue to haunt the civilized world. For the Christian, these evil forces have lost their ultimate power because they have been overcome in Christ's death and resurrection. Victory over them is available.[68]

C. In the occult world there is a tendency to downplay the mind and reason. For the Christian, the mind is to be used constructively in a faith context.

PART SEVEN
Conclusion

Representative N.C. groups have been presented. Secular and Christian evaluations have been made of each group. It should be helpful at this point to step back and see the N.C. movement in a broad perspective. In summary form, eight statements can be made about N.C. developments from a Christian perspective.

1. CHRISTIANS SHOULD NOT MINIMIZE THE CHALLENGE OF THE N.C. GROUPS

America's fascination with the East began in the early nineteenth century. Ralph Waldo Emerson and Walt Whitman talked much about Hinduism. The rise of theosophy and the Unity School of Christianity reflected the influence of Hindu teachings. The nineteenth and early twentieth-century interest in Eastern thought, however, was mostly confined to intellectuals and was centered largely in ideas.[1] It was only in the 1960s that an unprecedented interest in both Eastern and Western N.C. groups developed among lay people.

The crisis of Vietnam and disillusionment with American absorption in profit and power led many young people to revolt and reevaluation. The Western biblical heritage was undercut by such developments as the death of God movement. After finding the drug culture a dead end, the N.C. groups provided an alternative for many Americans.

As we have seen, the N.C. groups have weaknesses and limitations. In times of rapid change and crisis, however, few make a critical examination of options.[2]

It is ironic that as the West turns East, the East is turning West. Asians are involved in a strong emphasis on technology, Western political systems, and Western cultural forms. The East is becoming more activist and this-worldly.[3]

The N.C. groups, nevertheless, are challenging the materialistic, sensual, success-oriented, and over-rationalized Western way of life. Christians and other concerned Americans should not minimize the challenge.

2. BOTH CHRISTIANS AND N.C. LEADERS SHOULD BE FRANK AND OPEN ABOUT BASIC DIFFERENCES BETWEEN BIBLICAL CHRISTIANITY AND N.C. GROUPS

Our study of such groups as Zen Buddhism and Hare Krishna reveals

164

that these groups cannot be accommodated to the biblical world view. Zen Buddhism, for example, sees the self as an illusion. Zen teaches us how to escape the illusion of the ego. Another central idea of Zen is detachment. By eliminating the idea of self, Zen presents us with a detached way of life free from relationships. Hinduism teaches that the ultimate reality is unity with the impersonal Brahman.

The biblical teaching concerning sacrifice is a distinct alternative to the nonself and detachment emphasis of much Eastern thought. Christianity affirms that we are not to withdraw from others or use others, but give ourselves to others. The Christian is to sacrifice, love, and risk. Jesus Christ himself took the form of a servant for others and he is our model.[4]

3. CHRISTIANS CAN LEARN LESSONS FROM THE RISE OF N.C. GROUPS

A. An obvious lesson is that Christianity should avoid aligning itself too closely and uncritically with the currently dominant political and economic groups. The marketplace has importance in every society. But when Christianity aligns itself with those who see acquisition of gold as a faith or fetish, there is a danger involved.[5] A reaction against the greed of an acquisitive society can lead to a reaction against Christianity. In fact, this has happened in the West.

B. Protestants, as well as other religious groups, formerly saw devotional practices such as prayer and Bible reading as indispensable to the Christian life. The interest in the devotional practices of the N.C. groups points up the failure of most churches to teach their members practical techniques of spiritual discipline.[6]

C. The growth of N.C. groups has also reminded us that people hunger for simple human friendship and membership in a loving and caring community.

4. CHRISTIANS SHOULD SEEK TO CORRECT MISUNDERSTANDINGS ABOUT THE NATURE OF AUTHENTIC CHRISTIANITY

A. Authentic Christianity is not self-centered, an ego trip, or a withdrawal into the self. The biblical faith sees the self as essentially related to other selves, to God, and to a world of suffering and need. Christians do not seek to escape the world. Pain, distress, and confusion can be seen as potential sources for spiritual growth and change.[7]

B. Biblical Christianity does not necessarily encourage ruthless conquest and exploitation of nature. Scholars such as Frederick Elder show that the Bible undergirds a view of nature that involves restraint, qualitative living, and reverence for life.

5. The Challenge of the N.C. Groups Should Lead Christians to Recover and Restate the Breadth and Depth of the Christian World View

A. The biblical view of nature is important in the modern world. Although scientism is to be deplored, authentic science is important. The foundations for modern science have deep roots in the biblical teaching. The Bible states that nature is God's creation. The implication is that man is to discover nature's secrets and use them constructively for God's glory and man's good.

B. A significant Old Testament teaching concerns the observance of the sabbath. In the New Testament, an emphasis is made on the importance of worship and rest on the first day of the week. This biblical teaching about rest and worship embraces the truth of Eastern meditation and in addition furnishes a background for the Western emphasis on doing or action. A proper and regular observance of the sabbath or Lord's Day will give a person a continuing vision of God's purposes and furnish resources for daily living. Such a worship and rest day is not a withdrawal, but a plan which provides power and strength to live constructively in a needy world.[8]

6. In All Candor, Christians Should Point Out Basic Weaknesses of the N.C. Groups from a Christian Perspective

A. Even Eastern religious leaders criticize some of the N.C. groups which has radically altered their Hindu, Buddhist, or Islamic roots. In fact, certain N.C. groups are parodies of the broader religious movements they represent. The new groups seem to have been fabricated to satisfy the spiritual gluttony of the West. Classic Eastern views have been made into consumer commodities for Western markets by popular N.C. leaders.[9]

B. The day of *uncritical* acceptance of either the Christian or the New Consciousness view is passing. A more careful examination of the teachings of certain N.C. groups reveals that they have problems and flaws, and fail to meet many practical human and social needs.

C. New Consciousness groups are oftentimes used as getaways or escapes from life. Est is an example of a group which grafts insights into a program of ego-expansion and self-gratification. As a crossbreed of psychological and religious ideas and practices, est serves self-realization and narcissism.[10]

7. As a Religion that Emphasizes Being as Well as Thinking, Christianity Should Seek to Better Incarnate the Implications of the Christian Way

Much that is called Christian is the reflection of national, sectarian, and cultural conditioning which is often far from authentic Christian teaching. The biblical way of life calls for a constant renewal and reexamination of life patterns from the perspective of God's dynamic purpose revealed in Jesus Christ. The Christian faith further affirms that supernatural resources are available to help implement and incarnate this unprecedented and custom-shattering life-style.

8. In a Context of Religious Freedom and Openness of Commitment, Christianity Should Engage in a Program of Dialogue, Testing, and Witness

Syncretism or the combining of elements from various religious views is not a live option for the Christian. To assume that all religions are one is to rob each of the religions involved of seriousness.

All constructive religious dialogue must begin with a clear grasp of presuppositions. Key issues should be presented with openness, honesty, cross-questioning, and listening. According to Martin Buber, genuine dialogue does not call for compromise, but a willingness to listen, understand, and seek mutual enrichment. There should be reverence for reverence. Westerners have been accused of being both ignorant of other people's views and arrogant. Such a track record calls for people of the West to seek knowledge, display sympathy, and practice humility.

Although testing in religious dialogue has limitations, there is a place for establishing criteria for testing world views. Generally accepted criteria include comprehensiveness (does a view include all kinds of human experience?), inner intellectual coherence (does a view hang together?), and creativity (does it encourage renewal and the forward look?). The question of subjective satisfaction should be raised. When authentically practiced, does a given religious world view bring joy, happiness, and fulfillment? [11] Another way of testing involves the negative approach (which view has fewer difficulties?), and the positive question (which view answers more questions, corresponds with more facts, and explains experience as a whole better?).

The Christian ultimately falls back on his conviction that Jesus Christ is the one in whom all man's questionings find their final and fullest answer. Appreciation is given to every fragment of truth compatible with Christ's life and teaching. But for the Christian, those elements contrary to Christ, both in the Christian's own life and organizations or in the teaching of others, stand under judgment.

The enlightened Christian does not call for a return to the dogmatism and closed-system approach of earlier years. A significant contribution of the United States to the world is its teaching that it is possible and important to have an open society with open inquiry. Within such a society, each religious group has a right to witness to its faith or views.

Andrew Greeley, a Roman Catholic sociologist, maintains that it is in a society of pluralism and religious freedom that Christian orthodoxy is best maintained with intellectual virility and social vitality. It is also in a pluralistic religious society characterized by religious freedom that the Christian believer will have more and more contact with those who do not share his belief. In such an open society, the Christian has an opportunity to establish positive relations with what is constructive in alternate views. At the same time the Christian is free to step back and witness to his convictions.[12]

The dialogue-and-witness approach, which does not depend on official state or social pressure, challenges Christians to become so radiant, disciplined, and evangelical that people will see in their lives the Christian faith which they would commend. Persuasion, witness, and incarnation are utilized rather than official authority or mind-control methods.[13]

Heterogeneity and diverse religious views in a society can be seen as signs of vitality and excitement and as a spiritual challenge. In fact, an authentic religion based on reality should prosper in a context of openness and testing. Dialogue with divergent groups is oftentimes salutary. But the Christian is always ready to stand with a word of witness and prophetic challenge.

Notes

1. J. Stillson Judah, *Hare Krishna and the Counterculture* (New York: John Wiley & Sons, 1974), pp. 108 f.

2. Charles Y. Glock, "Consciousness Among Contemporary Youth: An Interpretation," ed. Charles Y. Glock and Robert N. Bellah, *The New Religious Consciousness* (Berkeley, California: University of California Press, 1976), p. 354.

3. Judah, *Hare Krishna and the Counterculture*, p. 188.

4. Edward A. Tiryakian, "Toward the Sociology of Esoteric Culture," ed. Edward A. Tiryakian, *On the Margin of the Visible* (New York: John Wiley & Sons, 1974), p. 275.

5. Judah, *Hare Krishna and the Counterculture*, p. 105.

6. Robert S. Ellwood, Jr., *Many Peoples, Many Faiths* (Englewood Cliffs, New Jersey: Prentice-Hall, Incorporated, 1976), pp. 275 f.

7. Ibid., pp. 277 f.

8. Ibid., p. 282.

9. Theodore Roszak, *Unfinished Animal* (New York: Harper & Row, Publishers, Incorporated, 1975), pp. 236 f.

10. Hal Lindsey, *The Terminal Generation* (Old Tappan, New Jersey: Fleming H. Revell Company, 1976), p. 88.

Part One

1. James W. Sire, *The Universe Next Door* (Downers Grove, Illinois: InterVarsity Press, 1976), p. 148.

2. Os Guinness, *The Dust of Death* (Downers Grove, Illinois: InterVarsity Press, 1973), pp. 196, 204.

3. Robert S. Ellwood, Jr., *Religious and Spiritual Groups in Modern America* (Englewood Cliffs, New Jersey: Prentice-Hall, Incorporated, 1973), p. 83.

4. Marvin Henry Harper, *Gurus, Swamis and Avatars* (Philadelphia: The Westminster Press, 1972), pp. 244, 248, 250.

5. Sire, *The Universe Next Door*, pp. 131 f.

6. R. D. Clements, *God and the Gurus* (Downers Grove, Illinois: InterVarsity Press, 1975), p. 10.

7. R. C. Zaehner, *The Convergent Spirit* (London: Routledge and Kegan Paul Limited, 1963), pp. 184–185.

8. Harper, *Gurus, Swamis and Avatars*, p. 12.

9. Guinness, *The Dust of Death*, p. 215.

10. Alan Watts, *Beyond Theology: The Art of Godmanship* (New York: Meridian Books, 1967), p. 32.

11. Sire, *The Universe Next Door*, p. 141.

12. Ibid., p. 135.

13. Harper, *Gurus, Swamis and Avatars*, pp. 26–27.

14. Ibid., p. 70.

15. Ibid., pp. 97–98.

16. Ibid., pp. 169–170.

17. Nathaniel Lande, *Mindstyles, Lifestyles* (Los Angeles: Price/Stern/Sloan, Publishers, Incorporated, 1976), p. 294.

18. Cf. Maharishi Mahesh Yogi, *Transcendental Meditation* (New York: New American Library, 1963).

19. "Who is This Man and What Does He Want?" (Berkeley, California: Spiritial Counterfeits Project, Incorporated, 1976). Cf. also Maharishi Mahesh Yogi, *Transcendental Meditation: The Science of Being and Art of Living* (Bergenfield, New Jersey: New American Library, 1963), pp. xii–xiii.

20. Jack Forem, *Transcendental Meditation* (New York: E. P. Dutton, 1973), pp. 204 ff.

21. "The TM Craze," *Time*, October 13, 1975, pp. 71–72.

22. Maharishi Mahesh Yogi, *On the Bhagavad-Gita: A New Translation and Commentary* (Baltimore: Penguin, 1969), p. 224.

23. Maharishi Mahesh Yogi, *Meditations of Maharishi Yogi* (New York: Bantam Books, 1973), pp. 17–18.

24. "Maharishi Over Matter," *Newsweek*, June 13, 1977, pp. 98, 100.

25. Gary E. Schwartz, "TM Relaxes Some People and Makes Them Feel Better," *Psychology Today*, April, 1974, p. 40.

26. Maharishi, *Meditation of Maharishi Yogi*, pp. 88 f.

27. Ibid., pp. 177, 178, 119, 123–124.

28. John R. Dilley, "TM Comes to the Heartland of the Midwest," and George E. LaMore, Jr., "The Secular Selling of a Religion," *Christian Century*, December 10, 1975, pp. 1129–1137.

29. Maharishi, *On the Bhagavad-Gita: A New Translation and Commentary*, p. 66.

30. William J. Preston, *Those Curious New Cults* (New Canaan, Connecticut: Keats Publishing, Incorporated, 1973), pp. 166–167.

31. "Who is This Man and What Does He Want?", p. 3.

32. David Haddon, "New Plant Thrives in a Spiritual Desert," *Christianity Today*, December 21, 1973, p. 12.

33. Judah, *Hare Krishna and the Counterculture*, p. 12.

34. Gregory Johnson, "The Hare Krishna in San Francisco," ed. Charles Glock and Robert Bellah, *The New Religious Consciousness*, p. 36.

35. J. Stillson Judah, "The Hare Krishna Movement," ed. Irving I. Zaretsky and Mark P. Leone, *Religious Movements in Contemporary America* (Princeton, New Jersey: Princeton University Press, 1974), p. 466.

36. Ibid., p. 466.

37. Ibid., p. 468 f.

38. Ibid., p. 464.

39. Stoner and Parke, *All God's Children*, p. 61.

40. Johnson, "The Hare Krishna in San Francisco," p. 50.

41. Judah, "The Hare Krishna Movement," ed. Zaretsky and Leone, *Religious Movements in Contemporary America*, p. 469.

42. Stoner and Parke, *All God's Children*, p. 140.

43. "The Hare Krishnas Today," (Spiritual Counterfeits Project).

44. Johnson, "The Hare Krishna in San Francisco," p. 39.

45. "The Hare Krishnas Today," (Spiritual Counterfeits Project).

46. Enroth, *Youth, Brainwashing and the Extremist Cults*, p. 25.

47. Johnson, "The Hare Krishna in San Francisco," p. 35.

48. Ibid., p. 36.

49. Ted Patrick, *Let Our Children Go!* (New York: E. P. Dutton & Company, Incorporated, 1976), p. 184.

50. Judah, "The Hare Krishna Movement," p. 468.

51. "The Freedom to Be Strange," *Time*, March 28, 1977, p. 81.

52. Ibid.

53. Judah, "The Hare Krishna Movement," p. 469.

54. Ibid., p. 468.
55. Stoner and Parke, *All God's Children*, p. 18.
56. Peterson, *Those Curious New Cults*, p. 147.
57. Gene Kieffer, "Kundalini: The Past in Your Future," ed. Martin Ebon, *TM: How to Find Peace of Mind Through Meditation* (New York: The New American Library, Incorporated, 1976), p. 190.
58. W. Edward Mann, *Orgone, Reich and Eros* (New York: Simon and Schuster, 1973), p. 140.
59. David Farren, *Sex and Magic* (New York: Simon and Schuster, 1975), pp. 91–92.
60. Mann, *Orgone, Reich and Eros*, p. 140.
61. Ellwood, *Many Peoples, Many Faiths*, p. 89.
62. Ibid., p. 90.
63. Ibid.
64. Benjamin Walker, "Kundalini," ed. Richard Cavendish, *Man, Myth & Magic, Volume 12* (New York: Marshall Cavendish Corporation, 1970), p. 1586.
65. Ibid.
66. Ellwood, *Many Peoples, Many Faiths*, p. 91.
67. Ralph Metzner, *Maps of Consciousness* (New York: Collier Books, 1971), p. 49.
68. Ellwood, *Many Peoples, Many Faiths*, p. 90.
69. Farren, *Sex and Magic*, p. 85.
70. Metzner, *Maps of Consciousness*, p. 50.
71. Nat Freedland, *The Occult Explosion* (New York: Berkley Medallion Books, 1972), p. 63.
72. Lande, *Mindstyles, Lifestyles*, p. 301.
73. Ellwood, *Religious and Spiritual Groups in Modern America*, p. 247.
74. Lande, *Mindstyles, Lifestyles*, p. 300.
75. Adam Smith, *Powers of Mind* (New York: Ballantine Books, 1975), p. 317.
76. Ibid., p. 321.
77. "Bubba Free John: An American Guru," (Berkeley, California: Spiritual Counterfeits Project, 1976). cf. Franklin Jones, *The Knee of Listening* (Los Angeles: The Dawn Horse Press, 1972), p. 135.
78. Ibid.
79. Ellwood, *Religious and Spiritual Groups in Modern America*, p. 250.

Part Two

1. Ellwood, *Many Peoples, Many Faiths*, p. 110.
2. Ibid., p. 115.
3. Ibid., pp. 116–117.
4. Ibid., p. 118.
5. Ibid., p. 114.
6. Ibid., p. 132.
7. Ibid., pp. 133–134.
8. Ibid., p. 201.
9. Ellwood, Robert S., Jr., *The Eagle and the Rising Sun* (Philadelphia: The Westminster Press, 1974), pp. 19–20.
10. Ellwood, *Many Peoples, Many Faiths*, p. 203.
11. Ellwood, *Religious and Spiritual Groups in Modern America*, p. 256.
12. Ellwood, *Many Peoples, Many Faiths*, p. 203.
13. Ibid., p. 204.
14. Hal Bridges, *American Mysticism from William Janes to Zen* (New York: Harper & Row, Publishers, Incorporated, 1970), p. 119.
15. Peterson, *Those Curious New Cults*, pp. 156–158.

16. Ellwood, *The Eagle and the Rising Sun*, p. 75. cf. also H. Neil McFarland, *The Rush Hour of the Gods* (New York: Harper Colophon Books, 1967), pp. 194–220.
17. Ibid., pp. 28–31.
18. Ellwood, *Religious and Spiritual Groups in Modern America*, pp. 268–271.
19. Ellwood, *The Eagle and the Rising Sun*, p. 88.
20. Ibid., p. 89.
21. Ibid., p. 91.
22. Ibid., p. 78.
23. Ibid., p. 94.
24. Ibid., pp. 96–100.
25. Ellwood, *Religious and Spiritual Groups in Modern America*, p. 273.
26. Ibid., p. 273.
27. "Happy Talk," *Newsweek*, June 5, 1972, p. 68.
28. Ellwood, *Religious and Spiritual Groups*, p. 270.
29. Ibid., p. 266.
30. *Time*, February 14, 1977, p. 84.

Part Three

1. Ellwood, *Many Peoples*, p. 312.
2. Ibid., pp. 316, 320.
3. Ibid., p. 318.
4. Ibid., p. 327.
5. Ellwood, *Religious and Spiritual Groups*, p. 254.
6. John A. Hutchison, *Paths of Faith* (New York: McGraw Hill Book Company, 1975), p. 480.
7. Geoffrey Parrinder, *Mysticism in the World's Religions* (New York: Oxford University Press, 1976), p. 124.
8. Ibid.
9. Kenneth Cragg, *The Call of the Minaret* (New York: Oxford University Press, 1956), p. 64.
10. Ibid., p. 64.
11. Ibid., p. 135.
12. Parrinder, *Mysticism*, p. 135.
13. Cragg, *The Call of the Minaret*, p. 65.
14. Parrinder, *Mysticism*, p. 130.
15. Ellwood, *Religious and Spiritual Groups*, p. 255.
16. Ellwood, *Many Peoples*, p. 232.
17. Ellwood, *Religious and Spiritual Groups*, p. 255.
18. Parrinder, *Mysticism*, pp. 133–134.
19. cf. Robert E. Ornstein, *The Mind Field* (New York: The Viking Press, 1976), pp. 103–135.
20. Peterson, *Those Curious New Cults*, p. 178.
21. Ibid., p. 170.
22. Ellwood, *Religious and Spiritual Groups*, p. 283.
23. Ibid., p. 285.
24. Peterson, *Those Curious New Cults*, p. 179.
25. Theodore Roszak, *Unfinished Animal* (New York: Harper & Row, Publishers, 1975), p. 138.
26. Peterson, *Those Curious New Cults*, p. 193.
27. Roszak, *Unfinished Animal*, p. 147.
28. Lande, *Mindstyles, Lifestyles*, p. 279.
29. Ellwood, *Religious and Spiritual Groups*, p. 162.
30. Roszak, *Unfinished Animal*, p. 147.
31. Ellwood, *Religious and Spiritual Groups*, pp. 162 f.

32. Peterson, *Those Curious New Cults*, p. 201.

33. Colin Wilson, *The Occult* (New York: Random House, 1971), p. 410.

34. Jacob Needleman, *The New Religions* (New York: Simon & Schuster, Incorporated, 1972), p. 107.

35. Ibid., p. 109.

36. Ibid., p. 110.

37. Ibid.

38. Christopher Evans, *Cults of Unreason* (New York: Dell Publishing Company, Incorporated, 1973), p. 223.

39. Ellwood, *Religious and Spiritual Groups*, p. 288.

40. Evans, *Cults of Unreason*, p. 224.

41. Needleman, *The New Religions*, p. 114.

42. Ibid., p. 106.

43. Ellwood, *Religious and Spiritual Groups*, p. 289.

44. Needleman, *The New Religions*, p. 118.

45. Ellwood, *Religious and Spiritual Groups*, p. 287.

46. Needleman, *The New Religions*, p. 118.

47. Ellwood, *Religious and Spiritual Groups*, p. 289.

48. Ibid.

49. Needleman, *The New Religions*, p. 111.

50. Smith, *Powers of Mind*, pp. 260–262.

51. Ibid., p. 259.

52. Ibid., pp. 257–260.

53. Ibid., pp. 254, 257.

54. Lande, *Mindstyles, Lifestyles*, p. 151.

55. Ellwood, *Religious and Spiritual Groups*, pp. 276 f.

56. Ibid., p. 277.

57. J. E. Esslemont, *Baha'u'llah and the New Era* (Wilmette, Illinois: Bahai Publishing Trust, 1944), p. 7.

58. Ellwood, *Religious and Spiritual Groups*, p. 277.

59. Ibid., p. 276.

Part Four

1. Ellwood, *Religious and Spiritual Groups*, p. 158.

2. "Getting Your Head Together," *Newsweek*, Sept. 6, 1976, p. 56.

3. Harriet Whitehead, "Reasonably Fantastic: Some Perspectives on Scientology, Science Fiction, and Occultism," ed. Zaretsky and Leone, *Religious Movements in Contemporary America*, pp. 557–558.

4. "A Sci-Fi Faith," *Time*, April 5, 1976, p. 57.

5. "A Farewell to Scientology?", *Newsweek*, Aug. 26, 1968, p. 8.

6. Joseph Martin Hopkins, "Scientology: Religion or Racket?", *Christianity Today*, November 7, 1969, p. 12.

7. Ibid., p. 6.

8. Donovan Bess, "Scientology: Total Freedom and Beyond," *The Nation*, September 29, 1969, p. 314.

9. Evans, *Cults of Unreason*, p. 22.

10. Ibid., p. 133.

11. "Have You Ever Been a Boo-Hoo?" *Saturday Evening Post*, March 21, 1964, p. 84.

12. Arlene and Howard Eisenburg, "The Dangerous New Cult of Scientology," *Parents Magazine*, June 1969, p. 82.

13. Peterson, *Those Curious New Cults*, p. 89.

14. "Scientology," *Life*, November 15, 1968, p. 103.

15. Ibid.

16. Lande, *Mindstyles, Lifestyles*, p. 129.

17. Ellwood, *Religious and Spiritual Groups*, p. 170.
18. Evans, *Cults of Unreason*, p. 36.
19. Whitehead, "Reasonably Fantastic," ed. Zaretsky and Leone, *Religious Movements in Contemporary America*, p. 576.
20. Evans, *Cults of Unreason*, p. 37.
21. Ibid., pp. 37 f.
22. Whitehead, "Reasonably Fantastic," p. 580.
23. Evans, *Cults of Unreason*, p. 41.
24. Ibid.
25. Ibid., pp. 43–44.
26. "A Sci-Fi Faith," *Time*, April 5, 1976, p. 57.
27. Evans, *Cults of Unreason*, p. 46.
28. Ellwood, *Religious and Spiritual Groups*, p. 170.
29. Evans, *Cults of Unreason*, p. 65.
30. Whitehead, "Reasonably Fantastic," p. 583.
31. Lande, *Mindstyles, Lifestyles*, p. 130.
32. Ellwood, *Religious and Spiritual Groups*, p. 172.
33. Whitehead, "Reasonably Fantastic," p. 586.
34. Ellwood, *Religious and Spiritual Groups*, p. 172.
35. Ibid., p. 176.
36. Lande, *Mindstyles, Lifestyles*, p. 129.
37. "Scientology," *Newsweek*, September 23, 1974, p. 84.
38. Lande, *Mindstyles, Lifestyles*, p. 129.
39. Ibid., p. 130.
40. "Scientology: Parry and Thrust," *Time*, July 25, 1977, p. 67.
41. Ellwood, *Religious and Spiritual Groups*, pp. 170 f.
42. Evans, *Cults of Unreason*, p. 130.
43. Whitehead, "Reasonably Fantastic," p. 548.
44. Ibid.
45. "A Sci-Fi Faith," *Time*, April 5, 1976, p. 57.
46. A. and H. Eisenberg, "The Dangerous New Cult of Scientology," p. 83.
47. Ralph Lee Smith, "Scientology—Menace to Mental Health," *Today's Health*, December, 1968, p. 34.
48. Ellwood, *Religious and Spiritual Groups*, p. 173.
49. "Scientology," *Life*, p. 100.
50. "To Be a Thetan," *The Economist*, Aug. 3, 1968, p. 40.
51. Smith, *Today's Health*, pp. 36–37.
52. Ron L. Hubbard, Scientology: *The Fundamentals of Thought* (Great Britain: Garden City Press Limited, 1968), p. 98.
53. *Time*, April 5, 1976, p. 57.
54. Lande, *Mindstyles, Lifestyles*, p. 128.
55. Hubbard, *Scientology*, p. 15.
56. Clay Steinman, "Scientology Fights Back, *The Nation*, May 22, 1972, p. 568.
57. Smith, *Today's Health*, p. 39.
58. Ibid., p. 38.
59. Hopkins, *Christianity Today*, p. 12.
60. Ibid., p. 12.
61. Stoner and Parke, *All God's Children*, p. 13.
62. Hopkins, *Christianity Today*, p. 12.
63. Peterson, *Those Curious New Cults*, p. 95.
64. Evans, *Cults of Unreason*, pp. 129 f.
65. Morton Marks, "Uncovering Ritual Structures in Afro-American Music," ed. Glock and Bellah, *The New Religious Consciousness*, p. 95.
66. Ibid., p. 100.

67. "Mind Control," Houston *Chronicle, Texas* Magazine, September 14, 1975, p. 8.
68. Jose Silva, *The Silva Mind Control Method* (New York: Simon & Schuster, 1977), p. 13.
69. Ibid., p. 22.
70. Ibid., p. 23.
71. Ibid., p. 24.
72. Harry McKnight, *Silva Mind Control Through Psychorientology* (Laredo, Texas: Institute of Psychorientology, Incorporated, 1972), p. 10.
73. Ibid., p. 17.
74. Silva, *The Silva Mind Control Method*, pp. 35–37.
75. Ibid., pp. 38–47.
76. Ibid., pp. 50–54.
77. Ibid., pp. 56–59.
78. Ibid., pp. 60–76.
79. Ibid., pp. 77–94,100–104.
80. Ibid., pp. 162 f.
81. Sam Merrill, "Under Mind Control," ed. Martin Ebon, *TM: How to Find Peace of Mind Through Meditation* (New York: New American Library, 1976), p. 114.
82. Silva, *The Silva Mind Control Method*, p. 116.
83. Elmer Green and Alyce Green, "How Safe Is 'Mind Training'?", ed. Martin Ebon, *The Satan Trap* (Garden City, New York: Doubleday & Company, 1976), pp. 249, 251.
84. Ibid., pp. 255 f.
85. Ibid., p. 256.
86. Margaret Gaddis, "Teachers of Delusion," ed. Ebon, *The Satan Trap*, p. 55.
87. Green and Green, "How Safe Is 'Mind Training'?" ed. Ebon, *The Satan Trap*, p. 257.
88. Ibid.
89. Ibid., p. 258.
90. Silva, *The Silva Mind Control Method*, pp. 105 f.
91. Ibid., pp. 106–107.
92. Ibid., pp. 108–109.
93. Ibid., p. 109.
94. Marks, "Uncovering Ritual Structures in Afro-American Music," ed. Glock and Bellah, *The New Religious Consciousness*, p. 102.
95. McKnight, *Silva Mind Control*, pp. 77–78.
96. Adelaide Bry, *est* (New York: Avon Books, 1976), p. 31.
97. Ibid., p. 150.
98. Ibid., p. 154.
99. Ibid., p. 153.
100. Ibid., p. 155. Cf. also Adam Smith, *Powers of Mind,* p. 269.
101. Robert A. Hargrove, *est: Making Life Work* (New York: Dell Publishing Company, 1976), p. 184.
102. Smith, *Powers of Mind*, p. 272.
103. "Getting Your Head Together," *Newsweek,* Sept. 6, 1976, p. 58.
104. Ibid.
105. Bry, *est*, p. 198.
106. Ibid., p. 199.
107. Smith, *Powers of Mind*, p. 287.
108. Bry, *est*, pp. 184–187.
109. "Getting Your Head Together," *Newsweek*, p. 58.
110. Bry, *est*, p. 189.
111. Ibid., p. 191.
112. Smith, *Powers of Mind*, p. 282.

113. "Getting Your Head Together," *Newsweek*, p. 58.

114. Hargrove, *est: Making Life Work*, pp. 156–157.

115. Kevin Garvey, "The Serpentine Serenity of est," *Christianity Today*, January 21, 1977, p. 15.

116. "Getting Your Head Together," *Newsweek*, p. 59.

117. Hargrove, *est: Making Life Work*, p. 45.

118. Lande, *Mindstyles, Lifestyles*, pp. 142–144.

119. Bry, *est*, p. 197.

120. Lande, *Mindstyles, Lifestyles*, p. 136.

121. Bry, *est*, p. 159.

122. Ibid., p. 32.

123. Smith, *Powers of Mind*, p. 278.

124. Bry, *est*, p. 164.

125. Ibid., p. 216.

126. Ibid., p. 33.

127. "Getting Your Head Together," *Newsweek*, p. 59.

128. Bry, *est*, p. 201.

129. Hargrove, *est: Making Life Work*, p. 235.

130. Bry, *est*, p. 204.

131. Ibid., p. 206.

132. Ibid.

133. Ibid., p. 208.

134. "est-erical Behavior?" *Newsweek*, May 9, 1977, p. 96.

135. Ibid.

136. Bry, *est*, p. 53.

137. Ibid., p. 209.

138. Ibid., p. 199.

139. Kevin Garvey, *Christianity Today*, p. 15.

140. "Secular Salvation: Life Change Through 'est' " *Christian Century*, November 10, 1976, p. 981.

141. Ibid., pp. 983–984.

142. "Est: Zen for the Bourgeois," (Berkeley, California: Spiritual Counterfeits Project).

143. Ibid.

144. Ibid.

145. Kevin Garvey, *Christianity Today*, p. 14.

146. Bry, *est*, p. 209.

Part Five

1. Ellwood, *Religious and Spiritual Groups*, p. 293.

2. Enroth, *Youth Brainwashing, and the Extremist Cults*, p. 100. Cf. also "The Way of the World," (Vol. VIII, #4, April, 1976) (Holy Spirit Association for the Unification of World Christianity, Incorporated, New York), p. 37.

3. Ibid. Cf. also "The Way of the World," p. 37.

4. J. Isamu Yamamoto, *The Moon Doctrine* (Downers Grove, Illinois: InterVarsity Press, 1976), p. 5.

5. Ibid., p. 6.

6. Ibid., p. 7.

7. James Bjornstad, *The Moon is Not the Son* (Minneapolis: Bethany Fellowship Incorporated, 1976), pp. 33–34.

8. Sun Myung Moon, *Divine Principle* (New York: The Holy Spirit Association for the Unification of World Christianity, Incorporated, 1977), p. 16.

9. Stoner and Parke, *All God's Children*, p. 57.

10. Ellwood, *Religious and Spiritual Groups*, p. 292.

11. Yamamoto, *The Moon Doctrine*, p. 8.

12. Lande, *Mindstyles, Lifestyles*, p. 265.
13. Bjornstad, *The Moon is Not the Son*, p. 36.
14. Ellwood, *Religious and Spiritual Groups*, p. 292.
15. S. Mark Heim, " 'Divine Principle' and the Second Advent," *Christian Century*, May 11, 1977, p. 449.
16. Cf. footnote 9.
17. Moon, *Divine Principle*, pp. 21,25–26.
18. Ibid., pp. 52–54.
19. Ibid., p. 66.
20. Ibid., pp. 70,72,78–79.
21. Ibid., pp. 79–80.
22. Ibid., pp. 459–463.
23. Ibid., pp. 423,424.
24. Ibid., pp. 140–141,171,210–212.
25. Ibid., pp. 147–148,151,182–183,360.
26. Ibid., p. 499.
27. Ibid., pp. 519–520.
28. Ibid., pp. 189–190.
29. Young Oon, Kim, *The Divine Principle and Its Application* (Belvedere Tarrytown, New York: The Holy Spirit Association for the Unification of World Christianity, n.d.), p. 196.
30. Moon, *Divine Principle*, pp. 188–190, 194,452.
31. In a public meeting at the University of Houston, Oct. 21, 1977, Neil Salonen, North American President of the Unification Church, stated, "Moon is our revelator. He could be the Messiah or Lord of Second Advent if he is successful and God ordains him in the near future."
32. "Sun Myung Moon Has Taken Our Daughter," *Eternity*, April, 1976, p. 30.
33. Enroth, *Youth, Brainwashing, and the Extremist Cults*, p. 110.
34. Moon, *Divine Principle*, pp. 533, 535.
35. Ellwood, *Religious and Spiritual Groups*, p. 293.
36. Ibid.
37. Stoner and Parke, *All God's Children*, pp. 195–196.
38. Enroth, *Youth, Brainwashing*, p. 111.
39. Stoner, and Parke, *All God's Children*, p. 180.
40. Ibid., p. 200.
41. Ibid., pp. 184–185.
42. Ibid., pp. 187–188.
43. Ibid., pp. 191–192.
44. Bjornstad, *The Moon Is Not the Son*, p. 20.
45. Yamamoto, *The Moon Doctrine*, p. 37.
46. Stoner and Parke, *All God's Children*, p. 146.
47. Ibid., p. 147.
48. "Honor Thy Father Moon," *Psychology Today*, January, 1976, p. 42.
49. Stoner and Parke, *All God's Children*, p. 117.
50. Ibid., pp. 118–119.
51. Bjornstad, *The Moon Is Not the Son*, p. 22.
52. Ibid., p. 21.
53. Robert J. Lifton, *Thought Reform and the Psychology of Totalism* (New York: W. W. Norton & Company, 1961).
54. Enroth, *Youth, Brainwashing*, p. 157.
55. Ibid., p. 160.
56. Ibid., pp. 160,162.
57. R. M. Kanter, *Commitment and Community* (Cambridge, Mass.: Harvard University Press, 1972), pp. 74–126.
58. Enroth, *Youth, Brainwashing*, p. 183.

59. Yamamoto, *The Moon Docrrine*, p. 24.

60. Ibid., p. 28.

61. Ibid., p. 22.

62. Bjornstad, *The Moon is Not the Son*, p. 72.

63. Enroth, *Youth, Brainwashing*, p. 206.

64. "Honor Thy Father Moon," *Psychology Today*, p. 45.

65. Stoner and Parke, *All God's Children*, p. 200.

66. Ibid., p. 5.

67. Smith, *Powers of Mind*, p. 214.

68. Heim, *Christian Century*, p. 453.

69. Honor Thy Father Moon," *Psychology Today*, p. 47.

70. Enroth, *Youth, Brainwashing*, p. 195.

71. Ibid., pp. 196–197.

72. Ibid., pp. 198–200.

73. Harvey Cox, *Turning East* (New York: Simon and Schuster, 1977), pp. 105–110, 158,165,167–168,174–175.

74. Evans, *Cults of Unreason*, p. 119.

75. Ibid.

76. Vincent Bugliosi, with Curt Gentry, *Helter Skelter* (New York: Bantam Books, 1975), pp. 636–637.

77. Evans, *Cults of Unreason*, p. 122.

78. Hans Holzer, *The New Pagans* (Garden City, New York: Doubleday & Company, Incorporated, 1972), pp. 62–63.

79. Ibid., p. 63. Cf. "On Love," *The Process*, North American Edition, n.d., p. 26.

80. "On Love," *The Process*, p. 8.

81. Bugliosi, *Helter Skelter*, p. 638.

82. Ibid., p. 637.

83. Ibid., pp. 638–639.

84. George Vandeman, *Psychic Roulette* (Nashville: Thomas Nelson Incorporated, 1973), p. 28.

85. George C. Bedell et al., "American Religion in Ferment," *Religion in America*, p. 493.

86. Ibid.

87. R. C. Zaehner, *Our Savage God* (New York: Sheet and Ward, Incorporated, 1974), p. 72.

88. Ibid., p. 293.

89. Richard Quebedeaux, *The New Charismatics* (Garden City, New York: Doubleday & Company, Incorporated, 1976), p. 196.

90. Ronald M. Enroth, Edward E. Ericson, Jr., C. Breckinridge Peters, *The Jesus People* (Grand Rapids, Michigan: William B. Eerdmans Publishing Company, 1972), p. 164.

91. Ibid.

92. Hiley H. Ward, *The Far-out Saints of the Jesus Communes* (New York: Associated Press, 1972), pp. 110–111.

93. Jack Sparks, *The Mind Benders* (Nashville: Thomas Nelson, Incorporated, 1977), pp. 227–228.

94. Ibid., p. 228.

95. Alan Wallerstedt, *Victor Paul Wierville and The Way* (Berkeley, California: Spiritual Counterfeits Project, 1976), p. 4.

96. Victor Paul Wierville, *Jesus Christ Is Not God* (New Knoxville, Ohio: The American Christian Press, 1975), p. 79.

97. Sparks, *The Mind Benders*, p. 194.

98. Ibid., pp. 198–199.

99. Wallerstedt, *Victor Paul Wierville*, p. 19.

100. Enroth, *Youth, Brainwashing*, pp. 87–89.

101. Ibid., p. 75.

102. Ward, *The Far-out Saints of the Jesus Communes,* p. 118.
103. Ibid., p. 119.
104. "The Holy Order of Mans," Spiritual Counterfeits Project, p. 2.
105. Enroth, Ericson, Peters, *The Jesus People,* p. 113.
106. Ibid., pp. 238–239.

Part Six

1. James W. Sire, *The Universe Next Door* (Downers Grove, Illinois: InterVarsity Press, 1976), pp. 156,183–184.
2. David Farren, *Living with Magic* (New York: Simon and Schuster, 1974), p. 213.
3. "Don Juan and the Sorcerer's Apprentice," *Time,* ed. Daniel C. Noel, *Seeing Castaneda* (New York: G. P. Putnam's Sons, 1976), p. 104.
4. Lande, *Mindstyles, Lifestyles,* p. 399.
5. Douglas McFerran, "The Castaneda Plot," *America,* February 26, 1977, p. 162.
6. "Don Juan and the Sorcerer's Apprentice," ed. Noel, *Seeing Castaneda,* p. 109.
7. Ibid., p. 99.
8. Sam Keen, "Sorcerer's Apprentice," ed. Noel, *Seeing Castaneda,* p. 77.
9. Ibid., p. 78.
10. *Time,* ed. Noel, *Seeing Castaneda,* p. 97.
11. Lande, *Mindstyles, Lifestyles,* p. 400.
12. Paul Riesman, "A Comprehensive Anthropological Assessment," ed. Noel, *Seeing Castaneda,* p. 51.
13. Elsa First, "Don Juan Is to Carlos Castaneda as Carlos Castaneda Is to Us," ed. Noel, *Seeing Castaneda,* p. 60.
14. *Time,* ed. Noel, *Seeing Castaneda,* p. 106.
15. *Esquire,* May 1971, p. 14.
16. McFerran, *America,* p. 162.
17. Sire, *The Universe Next Door,* p. 165.
18. *Time,* ed. Noel, *Seeing Castaneda,* pp. 106–107.
19. Carl Oglesby et al, "A Juanist Way of Knowledge," ed. Noel, *Seeing Castaneda,* pp. 165,166.
20. Ibid., p. 170.
21. Sire, *The Universe Next Door,* pp. 159–160.
22. Ibid., p. 160.
23. Ibid.
24. Ellwood, *Many Peoples, Many Faiths,* p. 44.
25. Sire, *The Universe Next Door,* p. 160.
26. Keen, ed. Noel, *Seeing Castaneda,* p. 81.
27. Ibid., p. 82.
28. Roszak, *Unfinished Animal,* pp. 248–249.
29. Oglesby, ed. Noel, *Seeing Castaneda,* p. 173.
30. Farren, *Living with Magic,* p. 266.
31. Carlos Castaneda, *Journey to Ixtlan* (New York: Simon and Schuster, 1972), pp. 291–302.
32. David Farren, *Sex and Magic* (New York: Simon and Schuster, 1975), p. 27.
33. Carlos Castaneda, *A Separate Reality* (New York: Simon and Schuster, 1971), p. 315.
34. Farren, *Sex and Magic,* p. 28.
35. Keen, ed. Noel, *Seeing Castaneda,* p. 75.
36. *Time,* ed. Noel, *Seeing Castaneda,* p. 96.
37. Keen, *Seeing Castaneda,* p. 85.
38. Keen, *Time,* ed. Noel, *Seeing Castaneda,* pp. 80, 101.
39. Ibid., pp. 86,101.
40. Farren, *Living with Magic,* p. 94.

41. R. C. Zaehner, *Mysticism, Sacred and Profane* (New York: Oxford University Press, 1971), pp. 198–207.

42. Geoffrey Parrinder, *Mysticism in the World's Religions* (New York: Oxford University Press, 1976).

43. Castaneda, *Journey to Ixtlan,* pp. 27–36.

44. Ibid., pp. 46–57.

45. Keen, *Seeing Castaneda,* p. 87.

46. Ibid., p. 81.

47. Sire, *The Universe Next Door,* pp. 155,192.

48. Farren, *Living with Magic,* p. 279.

49. Keen, *Seeing Castaneda,* p. 78.

50. Farren, *Living with Magic,* p. 215.

51. Ibid., pp. 215–216.

52. Ibid., p. 217.

53. Ibid., p. 216.

54. *Time,* ed. Noel, *Seeing Castaneda,* p. 109.

55. McFerran, *America,* p. 163.

56. Farren, *Living with Magic,* p. 264.

57. Wayne Oates, *The Psychology of Religion* (Waco, Texas: Word Books, 1973), p. 154.

58. Sire, *The Universe Next Door,* p. 176.

59. Ibid., p. 178.

60. Ibid., pp. 178–180.

61. Ibid., p. 61.

62. Ibid., p. 199.

63. Dennis Kinlaw, "The Demythologization of the Demonic in the Old Testament," ed. John Warwick Montgomery, *Demon Possession* (Minneapolis: Bethany Fellowship, Incorporated, 1976), p. 35.

64. *Time,* ed. Noel, *Seeing Castaneda,* p. 98.

65. Keen, *Seeing Castaneda,* p. 92.

66. Daniel C. Noel, "Don Juan as Messiah, Buddhist Master, Philosopher of the Unknown," ed. Noel, *Seeing Castaneda,* pp. 186–187.

67. James W. Boyd, "The Teachings of Don Juan from a Buddhist Perspective," ed. Noel, *Seeing Castaneda,* pp. 197 f.

68. Ibid., pp. 198–199.

Conclusion

1. Cox, *Turning East,* p. 9.

2. Ibid., p. 149.

3. Ibid., p. 101.

4. Ibid., pp. 87–89.

5. Ibid., p. 72.

6. Ibid., p. 64.

7. Ibid., pp. 77–78.

8. Ibid., pp. 65–66.

9. Ibid., pp. 133–134.

10. Ibid., p. 85.

11. Sire, *The Universe Next Door,* pp. 209–211.

12. Andrew Greeley, *Religion in the Year 2000* (New York: Sheed and Ward, 1969), p. 93.

13. Martin E. Marty, *Varieties of Unbelief* (New York: Holt, inehart and Winston, 1964).